Finding Peace in the Storm

Also by Dan Burke
from Sophia Institute Press:

Spiritual Warfare and the Discernment of Spirits
The Devil in the Castle
Into the Deep

Finding Peace in the Storm

Reflections on St. Alphonsus Liguori's
Uniformity with God's Will

by Dan Burke

*Translated from the Italian
of St. Alphonsus Liguori
by Thomas Tobin, C.Ss.R.*

**SPIRITUAL DIRECTION
SERIES**

SOPHIA INSTITUTE PRESS

Manchester, New Hampshire

Sophia Institute Press
Box 5284, Manchester, NH 03108
1-800-888-9344
www.SophiaInstitute.com

Sophia Institute Press is a registered trademark of Sophia Institute.

paperback ISBN 979-8-88911-026-2

ebook ISBN 979-8-88911-027-9

Library of Congress Control Number: 2023935422

First printing

*I want to thank my son Jordan
for regularly prodding me to read this great treatise
and for his diligent and noble pursuit of God.*

Perfection is founded entirely on the love of God:
"Charity is the bond of perfection"; and perfect love of God
means the complete union of our will with God's.

—St. Alphonsus Liguori

Contents

Finding Peace in the Storm

Introduction

During challenging times in the Church and in the world, one of the most powerful antidotes to spiritual and emotional desolation is the understanding and then the habitual awareness of God's healing and redemptive presence in the midst of chaos and suffering. This holy awareness provides insight into God's active work in the challenges we face and can give us hope, peace, and courage.

Even so, understanding is not enough. We must allow this understanding to lead us to the crossroads of sacred decisions. These decisions fix the trajectory of our souls and determine whether we will rise to the challenges of the storms of life or be overcome by them. In His mercy, God not only gives us the insight we need to know His presence and His will and the way of peace, but He also provides the strength and wisdom we need to find and walk the path of peace.

These sacred choices answer a very clear, simple question: Will we walk the path of peace and actively and deliberately embrace God's work and His will, or will we reject that path of peace and thus reject His will? A yes to the former will yield life and joy and serenity in the midst of even the most daunting of storms. The latter always yields a paralyzing cocktail of doubt, despair, and narcissism. The choice to embrace God's will leads the soul to a place where a transformational encounter with God is inevitable. The choice to resist God's will imprisons the soul in a dark, self-inflicted cell of torment, bitterness, anxiety, and separation from God.

A vital understanding of the sovereign hand of God in the midst of the storm comes through great works such as the one contained in the book you hold in your hands—St. Alphonsus Liguori's *Uniformity with God's Will*—Jean-Pierre de Caussade's *Sacrament of the Present Moment*, which was written around the same time as St. Alphonsus's book, and, more recently, Fr. Jacques Philippe's *Searching for and Maintaining Peace*, which reveals this powerful wisdom through another lens. The present book by St. Alphonsus covers some of the same ground as these others but is the most concise and sobering treatment available. At the same time, it is not lacking in depth of wisdom. It also has the benefit of coming from the pen of a Doctor of the Church.

One challenge the reader will encounter in this work is St. Alphonsus's black-and-white assertions and strong calls to conversion. These assertions are bold calls in the same vein as those offered by Jesus Himself. Modernism, under the guise of seeking to avoid offending weak consciences or commitments, always seeks to water down what it means to be an authentic disciple of Jesus. Yet Jesus' strong exhortations to perfection and righteousness could never be interpreted as insensitive to struggling souls. Instead, they served to awaken souls to holy desire and to inspire them to a higher order of living—a life of freedom and abundance in God.

These difficult challenges are meant to reveal where we truly stand in our progress in holiness. These calls to deeper union keep us from becoming complacent and self-satisfied. They humble us and reveal how lacking we are in our progress. If we are found wanting and are aware of this lack, we are not the recipients of condemnation. Instead, we have been given a gift, an opportunity to repent and turn more deeply to God.

Beyond the difficulty of standing in front of a holy mirror, we will also face a few more minor hurdles in this text. Because this book was written in the eighteenth century and then translated in the twentieth, the language can be archaic and difficult. Even so, the truths revealed through the heart and mind of this great saint are so important that we thought it wise to update the translation where helpful and to provide interpretive reflections and questions to deepen the reader's absorption of these life-changing truths. These additions are necessary not because of any deficiency in the teaching of St. Alphonsus but, rather, because his intended audience is so different from our modern readership. A lot has changed in the past few hundred years! We bring different perspectives, assumptions, and experiences to the text. One thing that hasn't changed, though, is the wisdom of St. Alphonsus. May this wisdom reach all in our time who desire to know the peace that passes all understanding (Phil. 4:7).

Modern readers should note that St. Alphonsus habitually excludes source references for Scripture quotes and those from other material. He simply assumes the reader knows what he is quoting from. I won't seek to remedy this habit except where it seems particularly helpful. My reflections are interspersed in his text but are easily distinguishable by a gray background. Questions for reflection and application are included at the end of each chapter.

My promise to you, dear reader, is this: if you read this treatise, meditate upon it, and make St. Alphonsus's thoughts your thoughts, the wind and waves of the storms of life, rather than dashing you against the rocks of despair, will become the means of your ascent up the narrow way to union with God in this life and in the next; and in this life, you will surely know peace in the midst of the storm.

—Dan Burke
Feast of St. Joseph

1

The Excellence of This Virtue

St. Alphonsus begins his holy treatise by assuming that we all should desire perfection and that the reader understands what that means. What does he mean by "perfection"? He means that state wherein we embrace and seek to live the highest expression of the good that God intends for us, in us, and through us. God's desire is that we be one with Him and that we know a state of peace and joy perpetually, regardless of circumstances—not that we can be perfect in the same way God is perfect but in the relative way that we can be in this life when we follow Him closely and thus become one with Him in will and desire.

Perfection is founded entirely on the love of God: *Charity is the bond of perfection*; and perfect love of God means the complete union of our will with God's: "The principal effect of love is so to unite the wills of those who love each other as to make them will the same things."

Said another way, when we love others deeply, we become more like them. We desire to emulate them—to be, in some way, absorbed into them. Thus, the love of a man and a woman leads them to Holy Matrimony, a joining of body and soul, in which the two become one. Married couples who are holy and equally yoked come to love the same things, desire the same things, pursue the same things together. In all of this, their love grows, their union grows, and their oneness grows. This does not mean they do not retain their individuality, unique likes and dislikes, attributes, and perspectives. Instead, it means that they seek to harmonize all of these goods with those of the beloved other. Thus, the love that each experiences grows as they continually pursue each other in love to give to each other in love. So it is with God and His most beloved creatures. This perfection that we seek and that He desires to give us enables us to become one with Him.

It follows, then, that the more one unites his will with the divine will, the greater will be his love of God. Mortification, meditation, receiving Holy Communion, and acts of fraternal charity are all certainly pleasing to God—but only when they are in accordance with His will. When they do not accord with God's will, He not only finds no pleasure in them, but He even rejects them utterly and punishes them.

To illustrate: A man has two servants. One works hard and diligently all day long but according to his own devices. The other, conceivably, works less, but he does what is requested of him. This latter, of course, is going to find favor in the eyes of his master; the other will not. Now, in applying this example, we may ask: Why should we perform actions for God's glory if they are not going to be acceptable to Him? God does not want sacrifices, the prophet Samuel told King Saul, but He does want obedience to His will:

Doth the Lord desire holocausts and victims, and not rather that the voice of the Lord should be obeyed? For obedience is better than sacrifices; and to hearken, rather than to offer the fat of rams. Because it is like the sin of witchcraft to rebel; and like the crime of idolatry to refuse to obey.

The astute reader here may protest, "But wasn't the sacrificial system established by God Himself? How, then, can this assertion be true that God doesn't want our sacrifices? If sacrifice is God's will, and it clearly is, isn't it obedience to God's will to offer sacrifice?" This is a challenging dilemma but one that Jesus helps us to clear up.

For the answer, we can look to Jesus in Matthew 7, where He works to correct this same problem in His disciples. He clearly sees that some who are following Him are doing so for the wrong reasons. He says to them (in general), "Let me show you what your final judgment will look like. You will call me *Lord*. You will have prophesied in my name. You will have cast out demons in my name. You will have done mighty works in my name." He then says, "I will say to you: Depart from me, I never knew you; depart from me, evildoers."

Here we have the same fundamental dilemma that St. Alphonsus proposes. Is it not God's will to call Jesus *Lord*? Is it not God's will to foretell and forthtell the truths of God? Is it not God's will to cast out demons and do mighty works in His name? The answer can be found in one word of this passage in the twenty-third verse: the word *knew*. The word in Greek is the same word that the Jews used to translate the love and union of Adam and Eve in Genesis ("Adam knew Eve"). Adam and Eve joined together because of their love. This joining was a union of love in the sacrament of Marriage, and this oneness produced an even deeper love: a knowing of each other, a desire to please and serve each other, an authentic union in love.

What Liguori and Jesus reveal is that, when we pursue "godly" or "religious" things that are truly and objectively good, but we are not motivated by love and an authentic desire to follow God and His will, then we are doing things from other, unhealthy motivations. How can this be so?

A few years ago, following a retreat that I gave at a parish, a woman who appeared to be in her sixties came up to me grinning from ear to ear. Let's call her Martha. Martha said to me with tears in her eyes, "I finally get it. I have been hiding in religious activities all my life. I am part of the altar society and this and that group in the parish. I do it all because I can't stand the silence. I work myself to death to avoid dealing with my wounds. I can see now that in all my religious activities, I have actually been hiding from God. I have come to realize that He wants to heal me. He wants my heart, not my scurrying around on the pretense that I am doing it all for love of Him. I do it to hide, not for Him. But I see it all so clearly now. He loves me. I want to love Him back. I want to give Him what time I have left but in a way that is truly worship of Him and not a hiding in my wounds."

Martha had a breakthrough that led to a true con-version. All her running around "for God" was really for her—to hide, to inebriate herself in activity. So God could rightly say to her, "I don't want all of your scurrying around in the parish doing all that 'good.' I want your heart." In all her activities, Martha was constructing a salvation of her own—one in which she was god and determined what was right and wrong. God was constantly calling her to allow Him to heal her, but she was rejecting that call. She didn't know Him because, until her conversion, she didn't want His love. She wanted her self-justification in anger and bitterness. Thus, if she were to die in that sin, she would have heard, "I don't know you." Did God want her to do good? Of course, but He wanted her to do it out of love of Him, not a false worship of self.

Martha's "good works" before she came to know and love God were not pleasing to Him. They were a very dangerous distraction from God. They didn't please God, because He didn't want the activity. He wanted Martha. Now she is in a place to come to know Him and to give herself to Him because she loves Him.

The man who follows his own will, independently of God's, is guilty of a kind of idolatry. Instead of adoring God's will, he adores his own in a certain sense. The greatest glory we can give to God is to do His will in everything. Our Redeemer came to earth to glorify His heavenly Father and to teach us by His example how to do the same. St. Paul represents Him saying to His eternal Father: *Sacrifice and offering You have not desired, but a body*

You have prepared for Me.... Then said I: "Lo, I come to do your will, O God." "You have refused the victims offered You by man; You will that I sacrifice my body to You. Behold I am ready to do Your will."

Our Lord frequently declared that He had come to earth not to do His own will but solely that of His Father: *I came down from Heaven, not to do my own will, but the will of Him that sent me.* He spoke in the same strain in the garden when He went forth to meet His enemies who had come to seize Him and to lead Him to death: *But that the world may know that I love the Father: and as the Father has given Me commandment, so do I; arise and let us go hence.* Furthermore, He said He would recognize as His brother those who would do His will: *Whosoever shall do the will of My Father who is in Heaven, he is My brother.*

To do God's will—this was the goal upon which the saints constantly fixed their gaze. They were fully persuaded that in this consists the entire perfection of the soul. Blessed Henry Suso[1] used to say, "It is not God's will that we should abound in spiritual delights, but that in all things we should submit to His holy will."

Here we have some clarity provided by the Most Zealous Doctor regarding the reality that we can do good things that are not pleasing to God because they are

---

[1] Blessed Henry Suso (1295–1366) was a German Dominican friar and mystic who was esteemed for his preaching and his spiritual direction.

not His will. This might prompt the question "How, then, can we know which good things we should do?" This question reveals that some confusion remains. A better question is "How can I come to know and love God and thus know how to honor Him with my life?" Authentic love is a challenge—it demands much of us. Knowing another, truly knowing them, is hard. It takes time and self-sacrifice. Jesus said, "My sheep know my voice, and I know them, and they follow me" (see John 10:27). How do we come to know this love and truly know His voice?

The first step is to cry out to God, as Martha did—to completely abandon our project of self-justification, the worship of our preferences and our desires, even if they are objectively good. The second step is to begin to immerse ourselves in the One whom we love little but want to love much. In the *Ascent of Mount Carmel*, St. John of the Cross gives a simple formula but one that is revolutionary in the souls who choose it: we must fall in love with Jesus. This love emerges in the soul through the loving discipline of mental prayer—a kind of pursuit of the heart that seeks to know Jesus, to follow Jesus, and to remain with Jesus every moment of our lives. (I will give you more specific help with this in the appendix "What Next?") St. Alphonsus knew this love well, and he wants us to know that same love. He reveals the right direction regarding how to hear God's voice as he points us to the great Doctor of prayer, St. Teresa of Ávila.

Teresa, of course, would call our attention to two life-altering spiritual disciplines. First, we must give ourselves to a daily practice of mental prayer rooted in the Gospels—in knowing and loving Jesus. This is where we will begin to know Him. Second, we must seek to conform ourselves to His will as it is revealed to us as we study Him, converse with Him, and come to truly understand Him and His will for us. We must, as St. John of the Cross exhorted, come to know Him, emulate Him, love Him, and follow Him. As we do this, we will begin to hear His voice ever more clearly. As we hear, we can better follow Him and give ourselves to Him in authentic love. Then our sacrifice and good works will be transformed into something that is pleasing to God and will help us get to Heaven.

The best way to do all of this—the path taken by every saint—is to immerse ourselves in Sacred Scripture, particularly the Gospels. This is where we come to know, hear, see, and engage Jesus in His incarnational glory. This is how we come to fall in love with Him.

"Those who give themselves to prayer," says St. Teresa of Ávila, "should concentrate solely on this: the conformity of their wills with the divine will. They should be convinced that this constitutes their highest perfection. The more fully they practice this, the greater the gifts they will receive from God, and the greater the progress they will make in the interior life."

A certain Dominican nun was given a vision of Heaven one day. She recognized there some people she had known during their mortal life on earth. She was told that these souls were raised to the sublime heights of the seraphs on account of the uniformity of their wills with that of God's during their lifetime here on earth. Blessed Henry Suso, mentioned above, said of himself: "I would rather be the vilest worm on earth by God's will, than be a seraph by my own."

During our sojourn in this world, we should learn from the saints now in Heaven how to love God. The pure and perfect love of God they enjoy there consists in uniting themselves perfectly to His will. It would be the greatest delight of the seraphs to pile up sand on the seashore or to pull weeds in a garden for all eternity, if they found out such was God's will. Our Lord Himself teaches us to ask to do the will of God on earth as the saints do it in Heaven: "Thy will be done on earth as it is in Heaven."

> This prayer, "Thy will be done," is properly understood to first mean, "Thy will be done in and through me."

Because David fulfilled all his wishes, God called him a man after His own heart: *I have found David … a man according to my own heart, who will do all my will.* David was always ready to embrace the divine will, as he frequently protested: *My heart is ready, O God, my heart is ready.* He asked God for one thing alone—to teach him to do His will: *Teach me to do Your will.* A single act of uniformity with the divine will suffices to make a saint.

Behold, while Saul was persecuting the Church, God enlightened him and converted him. What does Saul do? What does he say? Nothing else but to offer himself to do God's will: *Lord, what do You want me to do?* In return the Lord calls him a vessel of His choosing and an apostle of the Gentiles: *This man is a chosen instrument of mine, to carry my name before the Gentiles.*

He who gives his will to God, gives Him everything. He who gives his goods in alms, his blood in scourgings, his food in fasting, gives God what He has. But he who gives God his will, gives himself, gives everything he is. Such a one can say, "Though I am poor, Lord, I give You all I possess; but when I say I give You my will, I have nothing left to give." This is just what God does require of us: *My son, give me your heart.* St. Augustine's comment is: "There is nothing more pleasing we can offer God than to say to Him: 'Possess thyself of us.'" We cannot offer God anything more pleasing than to say: Take us, Lord, we give You our entire will. Only let us know Your will, and we will carry it out." If we would completely cause rejoicing in the heart of God, let us strive in all things to conform ourselves to His divine will. Let us strive not only to conform ourselves but also to unite ourselves to whatever dispositions God makes of us.

Conformity signifies that we join our wills to the will of God. Uniformity means more — it means that we make one will of God's will and ours, so that we will only what God wills; that God's will alone is our will. This is the summit of perfection, and to it we should always aspire. This should be the goal of all our works, desires, meditations, and prayers. To this end we should always invoke the aid of our holy patrons, of our guardian angels, and above all, of our mother Mary, the most perfect of all the saints because she most perfectly embraced the divine will.

Here St. Alphonsus speaks of our aspirations. St. Teresa of Ávila, in her great work *The Interior Castle*, argues that if we do not know that we can be one with God, we will not aspire to it. If we do not aspire to it, we will not pursue it. If we do not pursue it, we will not know it. Thus, our aspiration is the movement of our yes to God from inaction to action, from desire to prayer. This kind of prayer—"Show me Your will, Lord"—is a prayer that He always answers. It rarely comes in a moment like St. Paul's confrontation in Acts but is developed over time through a long, relentless commitment to Him in mental prayer, meditation, and listening. We begin this aspiration on our knees and then rise to action that reflects what He has revealed as we have come to know Him. As we kneel and rise in Him each day, His voice and His will become more and more clear to us.

Questions for Reflection

- What struck you or moved you in this chapter?
- Have you ever considered that your good works may, to an extent, be acts of self-worship and self-justification rather than true selfless worship of God? How so? What can you do to change that?
- How does the idea that at your judgment, you may hear, "I don't know you" strike you? What do you think needs to change so that you may hear, "Well done, good and faithful servant" (Matt. 25:21)?
- Has this chapter helped you to discover times when, while doing good, you were doing it for reasons other than for the love of God? If so, what were those reasons? Is this a pattern in your life? What can you do to change it?

2

Uniformity in All Things

Now that St. Alphonsus has prompted us to desire God's will and not our own, he turns a corner to a vital understanding of God's will as it is revealed in the daily circumstances of life. He posits that how we respond to what God has caused or allowed gives us an accurate understanding of how ready we are or how conditioned we are to receive what God is allowing or causing. If we discover we are not well disposed to His will, we have discovered something important about ourselves, and we must seek to heal. This is a moment suitable for gratitude rather than prideful self-criticism. It is a gift, not a punishment, to know what ails a patient. Whatever is revealed to the honest soul is by God's grace. And this revelation is His promise that if we will repent and turn to Him, He will heal us and show us the way.

The essence of perfection is to embrace the will of God in all things, prosperous or adverse. In prosperity, even sinners find it easy to unite themselves to the divine will; but it takes saints to unite themselves to God's will when things go wrong and are painful to self-love. Our conduct in such instances is the measure of our love of God.

Here the reader might guffaw. "It takes a saint! I am no saint! How can this be expected of me?" Of course, Alphonsus knows that it is God's will that we all become saints in this life. He simply assumes that we desire it and that God will make us saints as we seek to conform ourselves to His will.

When Alphonsus here speaks of things that "go wrong," he is, of course, speaking from a human perspective. Said another way, when circumstances are undesirable, we come to a true test of our willingness to accept what God is allowing or causing. To the degree that we embrace and respond to circumstances in a way that expresses a holy yes to God, we will be united with Him. To the degree that we bristle, brood, complain, or reject what is happening, as if it is outside the purview of God's loving hand, we are thereby separated from Him.

St. John of Ávila used to say: "One 'Blessed be God' in times of adversity is worth more than a thousand acts of gratitude in times of prosperity."

Often we assess ourselves based on those around us rather than on the higher standards of Jesus, Scripture, and the saints. This approach is dangerous, as it can bring a false comfort, depending on the company we usually keep. When we compare ourselves with the saints, however, we can no longer hide in mediocrity. Instead, we see that we are called to the heights of sanctity.

Furthermore, we must unite ourselves to God's will not only in things that come to us directly from His hands, such as sickness, desolation, poverty, and death of relatives, but likewise in those we suffer from others — for example, contempt, injustice, loss of reputation, loss of temporal goods, and all kinds of persecution. On these occasions, we must remember that while God does not will the sin, He does will our humiliation, our poverty, or our mortification, as the case may be.

The reader might be tempted to ask, "Why would God want me to experience humiliation?" The answer can be difficult to swallow. Above all, God wants us to know Him and love Him and to know that we are loved by Him for all eternity. Humiliation, adversity, and trials give us the opportunity to be purified by His healing hand. As we are purified, we are emptied of all that hinders our love for Him, our union with Him. Thus, these trials are a means to remove obstacles that prevent us from

fully knowing Him, His peace, and His joy in this
life and in the next.

It is certain and of faith that whatever happens, happens by the will of God: *I am the Lord forming the light and
creating the darkness, making peace and allowing adversity.*
From God come all things, good as well as the difficult.
We call adversities "evil"; actually, they are good and
meritorious, when we receive them as coming from
God's hands: *Shall there be evil in a city which the Lord
has not done? Good things and evil, life and death, poverty
and riches are from God.* It is true, when one offends us
unjustly, God does not will his sin, nor does He con-
cur in the sinner's bad will; but God does, in a general
way, allow for the material action by which such a one
strikes us, robs us, or does us an injury, so that God
certainly wills the offense we suffer, and it comes to us
from His hands.

A word of caution here is necessary. Older translations of Scripture, such as St. Alphonsus uses, use
the term *evil* to describe adversity. It is important
to note that while God allows adversity and even
sin, He is never the *author* of sin or evil. For us to
have the capacity to know, give, and receive love,
free will is necessary. Allowing free will means
also allowing evil, sin, and all that flows from the
sin-laden heart of man—good or bad.

Thus, the Lord told David that He would be the author of those things David would suffer at the hands of Absalom: *I will raise up evils against you out of your own house, and I will take your wives before your face and give them to your neighbor.* As well, God told the Jews that in punishment for their sins, He would send the Assyrians to plunder them and spread destruction among them: *The Assyrian is the rod and staff of my anger.... I will send him to take away the spoils.* "Assyrian wickedness served as God's scourge for the Hebrews" is St. Augustine's comment on this text. And our Lord Himself told St. Peter that His sacred Passion came not so much from man as from His Father: *The chalice which my Father has given me, shall I not drink it?*

When the messenger came to announce to Job that the Sabeans had plundered his goods and slain his children, he said: *The Lord gives and the Lord takes away.* He did not say: "The Lord has given me my children and my possessions, and the Sabeans have taken them away." He realized that adversity had come upon him by the will of God. Therefore, he added: *As it has pleased the Lord, so is it done. Blessed be the name of the Lord.* We must not, therefore, consider the afflictions that come upon us as happening by chance or solely from the malice of men; we should be convinced that what happens, happens by the will of God.

Apropos of this, it is related that two martyrs, Epictetus and Atho, being put to torture by having their bodies raked with iron hooks and burned with flaming torches, kept repeating: "Work Thy will upon us, O Lord." Arrived at the place of execution, they exclaimed: "Eternal God, be blessed in that Your will has been entirely accomplished in us." Cesarius points out what we have been saying by offering this incident in the life of a certain monk: Externally, his religious observance was the same as that of the other monks, but he had attained such sanctity that the mere touch of his garments healed the sick. Marveling at these deeds, since his life was no more exemplary than the lives of the other monks, the superior asked him one day what was the cause of these miracles. He replied that he, too, was mystified and was at a loss how to account for such happenings.

"What devotions do you practice?" asked the abbot.

He answered that there was little or nothing special that he did beyond making a great deal of willing only what God willed, and that God had given him the grace of abandoning his will totally to the will of God. "Prosperity does not lift me up, nor adversity cast me down," added the monk. "I direct all my prayers to the end that God's will may be done fully in me and by me."

"That raid that our enemies made against the monastery the other day, in which our stores were plundered, our granaries put to the torch, and our cattle driven off—did not this misfortune cause you any resentment?" queried the abbot.

"No, Father," came the reply. "On the contrary, I returned thanks to God—as is my custom in such circumstances—fully persuaded that God does all things, or permits all that happens, for His glory and for our greater good; thus I am always at peace, no matter what happens."

Seeing such uniformity with the will of God, the abbot no longer wondered why the monk worked so many miracles.

It is worth emphasizing what this holy monk reveals as the fruit of this disposition toward the will of God: "Thus I am at peace no matter what happens." Can we claim that we have that same peace, which passes all understanding? If not, it is likely because we reject the will of God rather than embrace it.

Unlike the responses of this holy monk, our reactions to the challenges of the world and in the Church can compel us to see only through a lens that excludes the sovereign action of God and allows our mere human will (or the demonic, which works silently on the human will) to determine how and why things happen. When we rail, criticize, and obsess over the work of our "enemies," or of the enemies of all that is good and true in the Church, we can find ourselves in the very dangerous position of railing at something that God has allowed—and thus at God Himself. Instead, we should ask ourselves, "What is the Almighty doing here? How can I join Him? How can I ease the suffering of His people? How can I be part of the solution to the difficulties at hand and thus bring the joy and redemptive hand of God to bear in the midst of this darkness?"

With respect to St. Alphonsus's pointing to our problematic focus on the "malice of men," when we see only "conservative" and "liberal" scheming both within and outside the Church, and we fail to see the presence of God in our midst, we can easily fall into wrath and despair and the wailing and gnashing of teeth.

If we would but lift our eyes above the fray and ask, "What are You doing, Lord?" and "How can I join You?," we will instead become lights in the darkness. We will be, like this monk, a means of healing and witnesses to the holy and transcendent peace that comes when we truly know God. And others will be drawn to this authentic relationship with the One who, in all things, seeks to heal and restore all that is truly good.

Questions for Reflection

- What stood out, struck you, or moved you in this chapter?
- Have you allowed yourself to fall into the trap of seeing the challenges in the Church and in the world only through a political lens? What can you do to change that?
- Are there some areas in which you find it easier to accept the will of God and other areas in which you find it harder? Why do you think the harder areas make it so difficult for you?
- St. Alphonsus asserts that your conduct in difficulty is the measure of your love for God. What does your conduct in difficulty reveal about you and your love for God? Is God asking you to change something in the way you see and respond to life as it unfolds around you?

3

Happiness Deriving from Perfect Uniformity

Acting according to this pattern, one not only becomes holy but also enjoys perpetual serenity in this life. Alphonsus the Great, king of Aragon, being asked one day whom he considered the happiest person in the world, answered: "He who abandons himself to the will of God and accepts all things, prosperous and adverse, as coming from His hands." *To those that love God, all things work together unto good.* Those who love God are always happy, because their whole happiness is to fulfill, even in adversity, the will of God. Afflictions do not mar their serenity, because by accepting misfortune, they know they give pleasure to their beloved Lord: *Whatever shall befall the just man, it shall not make him sad.*

This statement is quite remarkable. It is worth asking: How does a man with perspective like this see God? It is clear that his love is strong, but there is more here. There is a deep trust in the goodness of God—in the reality that He loves us so profoundly that He is even willing to allow extremely difficult things to assail us for the purpose of our freedom, our healing, and our salvation.

Modern parenting often takes the exact opposite approach, as if making life easy for children is a good thing. In fact, most drug-rehab facilities are filled with children of wealthy parents who sought to protect those children from the very adversity they needed to shape their souls and their character. Those children are now imprisoned by weak minds, hearts, and wills that cannot think and act in ways that allow for freedom. When we protect our children from consequences, we protect them from learning, growing, and becoming men and women of strength and integrity.

In contrast, our heavenly Father loves us in a way that would never allow Him to protect us from that which we need for our salvation. Understanding this about His character, we can rest assured that all we encounter is necessary for the fulfillment of all the good that our hearts desire.

Indeed, what can be more satisfactory to a person than to experience the fulfillment of all his desires? This is the happy lot of the man who wills only what God wills, because everything that happens, save sin, happens through the will of God. There is a story to this effect in the *Lives of the Fathers* about a farmer whose crops were more plentiful than those of his neighbors. On being asked how this happened with such unvarying regularity, he said he was not surprised because he always had the kind of weather he wanted. He was asked to explain. He said: "It is so because I want whatever kind of weather God wants, and because I do, He gives me the harvests I want." If souls resigned to God's will are humiliated, says Salvian,[2] they want to be humiliated; if they are poor, they want to be poor; in short, whatever happens is acceptable to them; hence, they are truly at peace in this life. In cold and heat, in rain and wind, the soul united to God says: "I want it to be warm, to be cold, windy, to rain, because God wills it."

This is the beautiful *freedom of the sons of God*, and it is worth vastly more than all the rank and distinction of blood and birth, more than all the kingdoms in the world. This is the abiding peace that, in the experience of the saints, *surpasses all understanding*. It surpasses all pleasures rising from gratification of the senses, from social gatherings, banquets, and other worldly amusements; vain and deceiving as they are, they captivate the senses for a moment but bring no lasting contentment; rather, they afflict man in the depth of his soul, where alone true peace can reside.

Here St. Alphonsus references a truly astonishing passage from St. Paul in his letter to the Philippians:

Rejoice in the Lord always; again I will say, rejoice. Let all men know your forbearance.

[2] Salvian was a fifth-century priest and writer in Roman Gaul.

The Lord is at hand. Have no anxiety about
anything, but in everything by prayer and sup-
plication with thanksgiving, let your requests be
made known to God. And the peace of God,
which passes all understanding, will keep your
hearts and your minds in Christ Jesus. (4:4–7)

The most astonishing aspect of this passage is that
it was written while Paul was in prison! The only right
he retained was to have a trial before Caesar. He had
given all up for Christ, and now nothing remained
for him. Yet he was able, in the midst of what most
would call a profound tragedy, to rejoice and speak of
supernatural peace.

How can he say, "Have no anxiety about anything"?
He could say it because he clearly knew Jesus. Paul
was walking in the will of God, and God would never
lead him astray. Thus, he had the peace that passes
all understanding because he entrusted himself to his
faithful and trustworthy Father in Heaven and embraced His holy will. This kind of embrace is the most
powerful source of peace a man can know in the face
of all that can and will assault us in this life.

Solomon, who tasted to saturation all the pleasures
of the world and found them bitter, voiced his disillu-
sionment thus: *But this also is vanity and vexation of spirit.
A fool*, says the Holy Spirit, *is changed as the moon; but a
holy man continues in wisdom as the sun.* The fool—that is,
the sinner—is as changeable as the moon, which today

waxes and tomorrow wanes; today he laughs, tomorrow he cries; today he is meek as a lamb, tomorrow cross as a bear. Why? Because his peace of mind depends on the prosperity or the adversity he meets; he changes with the changes in the things that happen to him.

The just man is like the sun, constant in his serenity, no matter what happens to him. His calmness of soul is founded on his union with the will of God; hence, he enjoys unruffled peace. This is the peace promised by the angel of the Nativity: *And on earth, peace to men of good will.* Who are these "men of good will" if not those whose wills are united to the infinitely good and perfect will of God? "The good, and the acceptable, and the perfect will of God." By uniting themselves to the divine will, the saints have enjoyed paradise by anticipation in this life.

It is worth asking the following question and taking a moment to imagine the answer: *What would it be like to know this complete peace in the midst of any storm?* Do we even believe it is possible? How would this reality change the way we think and act? What effect would our change in behavior have on us and on others?

The idea of peace in the midst of the storm is compelling to all of us, but it can sometimes seem so far out of reach. To help you understand the foundational spiritual disciplines necessary to know this peace, I have added the appendix "What Next?" at the end of this book. It provides resources for you to take concrete steps toward knowing the peace that St. Alphonsus reveals here and that Jesus has promised. In this book, we are gaining invaluable clarity regarding truths about God and about us. What we often need are practical steps we can take to ultimately and fully know and embrace the truth that will truly set us free.

Accustoming themselves to receive all things from the hands of God, says St. Dorotheus,[3] the men of old maintained continual serenity of soul. St. Mary Magdalene of Pazzi[4] derived such consolation at hearing the words *will of God* that she usually fell into an ecstasy of love. The instances of jangling irritation that are bound to arise will not fail to make surface impact on the senses. This, however, will be experienced only in the inferior part of the soul; in the superior part will reign peace and tranquility as long as our will remains united with God's. Our Lord assured His apostles: *Your joy no man shall take from you.... Your joy shall be full.* He who unites his will to God's experiences a full and lasting joy: full, because he has what he wants, as was explained above; lasting, because no one can take his joy from him, since no one can prevent what God wills from happening.

---

[3] Possibly the sixth-century monk St. Dorotheus of Gaza.
[4] St. Mary Magdalene of Pazzi (1566–1607) was an Italian Carmelite nun who received many ecstasies and graces from God.

Here Alphonsus reveals a truth that we can easily overlook or misunderstand in our experience. He notes that those living in habitual peace are not immune to irritations that surface in the senses. He also asserts, however, that when we fully embrace God's will, these stirrings of our lower nature are not strong enough to dominate or overtake us. God remains our strength and our shield as we face the storm, even if the storm is strong enough to rattle us a bit. So yes, we will always be human and feel or experience some measure of fear, anxiety, sadness, and so on. But to what degree? The hearts and minds of those who walk close to the Lord find rest and refuge in His care, rather than being overcome by whatever assails them.

The devout Fr. John Tauler[5] relates this personal experience: For years he had prayed God to send him someone who would teach him the real spiritual life. One day, at prayer, he heard a voice saying: "Go to such-and-such a church, and you will have the answer to your prayers." He went, and at the door of the church he found a beggar, barefoot and in rags. He greeted the mendicant, saying, "Good day, my friend."

"Thank you, sir, for your kind wishes, but I do not recall ever having had a 'bad' day."

"Then God has certainly given you a very happy life."

---

[5] John Tauler (1300–1361) was a German Dominican and mystic.

"That is very true, sir. I have never been unhappy. In saying this, I am not making any rash statement either. This is the reason: When I have nothing to eat, I give thanks to God; when it rains or snows, I bless God's providence; when someone insults me, drives me away, or otherwise mistreats me, I give glory to God. I said I've never had an unhappy day, and it's the truth, because I am accustomed to will unreservedly what God wills. Whatever happens to me, sweet or bitter, I gladly receive from His hands as what is best for me. Hence my unvarying happiness."

"Where did you find God?"

"I found Him where I left creatures."

"Who are you anyway?"

"I am a king."

"And where is your kingdom?"

"In my soul, where everything is in good order; where the passions obey reason, and reason obeys God."

"How have you come to such a state of perfection?"

"By silence. I practice silence toward men while I cultivate the habit of speaking with God."

This holy man provides some practical advice we can grab hold of. It can be summarized in the simple idea of praising God in all things. This is certainly harder than it sounds because it requires a fundamental disposition of gratitude. One way of cultivating this disposition is to adopt the practice of praising God for at least three things every evening as part of our nightly examen. This is a normative practice for members of the community of Apostoli Viae.[6]

It is easy to be thankful for pleasant and easy circumstances. To reach deeper levels of sanctity, we might thank God for the hardest things in our day as well as those things that brought us consolations.

"Conversing with God is the way I found and maintain my peace of soul." Union with God brought this poor beggar to the very heights of perfection. In his poverty he was richer than the mightiest monarch; in his sufferings, he was vastly happier than worldlings amid their worldly delights.

Here we have what I believe to be a purposeful repetition of a key secret in the path to peace and union with God—mental prayer. This holy beggar said that he had a "habit of speaking with God." "Speaking with God" is certainly an apt description of mental prayer. This approach to prayer is the most efficacious path to knowing, loving, and emulating Jesus. In fact, St. Alphonsus has boldly asserted, in his great work *Prayer: The Great Means of Salvation and Perfection*, that one must practice mental prayer in order to make it to Heaven. So here he plants the seed again. Do we desire to

[6] Apostoli Viae is a private association of the faithful that teaches the contemplative life to lay, religious, and priests. You can find out more at ApostoliViae.org.

know this peace and union with God? We must learn to pray—not superficial prayer that only asks for things but a prayer of union that is a holy exchange of love between creature and Creator. This love is why we were brought into existence. If we give ourselves to this prayer, if we make it a priority, we will know God in and through this prayer, and we will know the peace that comes with this vital union of grace.

Questions for Reflection

- What stood out, struck you, or moved you in this chapter?
- Do you trust God to care for your soul, your needs, and the needs of your family, or does anxiety plague your heart when you face threatening circumstances? If you lack trust in God, why is that? What can you do about it?
- Do you struggle with anxiety and negative thoughts, or are you normally filled with peace? If you do struggle with anxiety, how can you allow God to heal you?
- When you pray, how do you begin your conversation with God? Do you speak His name? Do you greet Him? Do you talk with Him as a loving Father or a trustworthy friend?
- Do you practice daily mental prayer in order to know, love, and follow Jesus more closely? If so, is it fruitful for you? If you don't yet practice mental prayer or you are not sure what it is, look at the appendix "What Next?" where you will find ample resources to help you begin this vital journey to peace.

4

God Wills Our Good

To say that "God wills our good" is the same as to say that "all that God wills is ultimately for His glory, our good, and our salvation." He desires that we spend eternity in perfect love and peace with Him. He desires to lead us to Heaven, where we will discover the final end of all tears, sadness, sin, and despair. He desires that we know pure and perfect love without end. But we must embrace the pathway to this great love. We must embrace His will and His ways and never resist them.

Oh, the supreme folly of those who resist the divine will! In God's providence, no one can escape hardship: *Who resists His will?* A person who rails at God in adversity suffers without merit; moreover, by his lack of resignation, he adds to his punishment in the next life and experiences greater disquietude of mind in this life: "Who resists him and has had peace?" The screaming rage of the sick man in his pain, the whining complaints of the poor man in his destitution—what will they avail these people, except increase their unhappiness and bring them no relief?

"Little man," says St. Augustine, "grow up. What are you seeking in your search for happiness? Seek the one Good that embraces all others." Whom do you seek, friend, if you seek not God? Seek Him, find Him, cleave to Him; bind your will to His with bands of steel, and you will live always at peace in this life and in the next. God wills only our good; God loves us more than anybody else can or does love us. His will is that no one should lose his soul, that everyone should save and sanctify his soul: *Not willing that any should perish, but that all should return to penance. This is the will of God, your sanctification.* God has made the attainment of our happiness His glory. Since He is, by His nature, infinite goodness, and since, as St. Leo says, goodness is generous in self-giving, God has a supreme desire to make us sharers of His goods and of His happiness.

If, then, He sends us suffering in this life, it is for our own good: *All things work together unto good.* Even chastisements come to us not to crush us but to make us mend our ways and save our souls: "Let us believe that these scourges of the Lord have happened for our amendment and not for our destruction." God surrounds us with His loving care lest we suffer eternal damnation: *O Lord, Thou hast crowned us as with a shield of Thy good will.* He is most attentive to our welfare:

The Lord is solicitous for me. What can God deny us when He has given us His own Son? *He that spared not even His own Son, but delivered Him up for us all, how has He not also, with Him, given us all things?* Therefore, we should most confidently abandon ourselves to all the dispositions of divine providence, since they are for our own good. In all that happens to us, let us say: *In peace, in the selfsame I will sleep, and I will rest: Because You, O Lord, have singularly settled me in hope.* Let us place ourselves unreservedly in His hands because He will not fail to care for us:

Cast all your cares upon Him, for He cares for you. Let us keep God in our thoughts and carry out His will, and He will think of us and of our welfare. Our Lord said to St. Catherine of Siena, "Daughter, think of Me, and I will always think of you." Let us often repeat with the spouse in the Canticle: *My beloved to me, and I to him.* St. Niles, abbot, used to say that our petitions should be not that our wishes be done but that God's holy will should be fulfilled in us and by us. When, therefore, something difficult happens to us, let us accept it from His hands, not only patiently, but even with gladness, as did the apostles *who went from the presence of the council rejoicing, that they were accounted worthy to suffer for the name of Jesus.*

A notable omission here points to St. Alphonsus's assumption that we are familiar with the passage regarding the apostles and suffering. What treatment at the council were the disciples rejoicing over? Chapter 5 of the Acts of the Apostles reveals that they were severely beaten for preaching the gospel. These kinds of beatings often resulted in death. The backs of the disciples were no doubt a bloody mess as their clothing clung to their open wounds. They seemed to have no concern over this unjust treatment but instead rejoiced.

Remember Paul's admonition from prison regarding the peace that passes all understanding? Here we have joy that passes all understanding. It is a joy that can come only from knowing God's pleasure and what it means to follow His will and thereby know Him in ways that would otherwise be impossible. In this instance, the disciples shared in the sufferings of Jesus because they embraced their suffering for His sake and because they were confident that they were fulfilling His holy will.

What greater consolation can come to a soul than to know that by patiently bearing some tribulation, it gives God the greatest pleasure in its power? Spiritual writers tell us that though the desire of certain souls to please God by their sufferings is acceptable to Him, still more pleasing to Him is the union of certain others with His will, so that their will is neither to rejoice nor to suffer but to hold themselves completely amenable to His will, and they desire only that His holy will be fulfilled. If, devout soul, it is your will to please God and live a life of serenity in this world, unite yourself always and in all things to the divine will. Reflect that all the sins of your past wicked life happened because you wandered from the path of God's will. For the future, embrace God's good pleasure and say to Him in every happening: *Yes, Father, for so it has seemed good in Your sight.* When anything disagreeable happens, remember it comes from God and say at once, "This comes from God" and be at peace: *I was dumb and opened not my mouth because You have done it.* Lord, since You have done this, I will be silent and accept it.

Direct all your thoughts and prayers to this end: to beg God constantly in meditation, Communion, and visits to the Blessed Sacrament that He help you accomplish His holy will.

> Here St. Alphonsus offers us very practical advice. When we pray, when we visit Him in the Blessed Sacrament, we should beg God to help us to embrace His will. How can we do this? A simple fervent prayer will suffice: "Lord, I know that You love me and that all You will is for my good. Please help me to embrace Your will and thus to know union with You and peace in this life and in the next."

Form the habit of offering yourself frequently to God by saying, "My God, behold me in Your presence. Do with me, and all that I have, as is pleasing to you."

> We can also adapt another prayer derived from St. Alphonsus's meditations on the Stations of the Cross: "I love You, Jesus my love; grant that I might love You always, and do with me what You will."

This was the constant practice of St. Teresa. At least fifty times a day, she offered herself to God, placing herself at His entire disposition and good pleasure. How fortunate you, kind reader, if you, too, act thus! You will surely become a saint. Your life will be calm and peaceful; your death will be happy. At death, all our hope of salvation will come from the testimony of our conscience as to whether or not we are dying resigned to God's will. If during life we have embraced everything as coming from God's hands, and if at death we embrace death in fulfillment of God's holy will, we shall certainly save our souls and die the death of saints. Let us, then, abandon everything to God's good pleasure, because being infinitely wise, He knows what is best for us; and being all-good and all-loving — having given His life for us — He wills what is best for us. Let us, as St. Basil counsels us, rest secure in the conviction that beyond the possibility of a doubt, God works to bring about what is best for us and what is infinitely better than we could ever hope to accomplish or desire ourselves.

Questions for Reflection

- What stood out, struck you, or moved you in this chapter?
- Have you ever become stuck in a cycle of complaining about illness or some other difficult circumstances? How so? What can you do to change that pattern?
- Do you have a sense of how you have resisted God's will in the past? How so? How can you avoid repeating the same mistake in the future?
- How does the phrase "God has made the attainment of our happiness His glory" strike you? Does it ring true? If not, why?
- Write your own prayer of surrender to God's will in whatever way is most meaningful to you. Keep it close at hand and repeat it regularly.

5

Special Practices of Uniformity

Let us now take up in a practical way the consideration of those matters in which we should unite ourselves to God's will.

1. *In external matters.* In times of great heat, cold, or rain; in times of famine, epidemics, and similar occasions, we should refrain from expressions like these: "What unbearable heat!" "What piercing cold!" "What a tragedy!" In these instances, we should avoid expressions indicating opposition to God's will. We should want things to be just as they are because it is God who thus desires them. An incident in point would be this one: Late one night, St. Francis Borgia arrived unexpectedly at a Jesuit house, in a snowstorm. He knocked and knocked on the door, but all to no purpose because, the community being asleep, no one heard him. When morning came, all were embarrassed for the discomfort he had experienced by having had to spend the night in the open. The saint, however, said he had enjoyed the greatest consolation

during those long hours of the night by imagining that he saw our Lord up in the sky dropping the snowflakes down upon him.

2. *In personal matters.* In matters that affect us personally, let us deliberately embrace God's will. For example, in hunger, thirst, poverty, desolation, loss of reputation, let us always say: "Build up or tear down, O Lord, as seems good in Your sight. I am content. I wish only what You desire." Thus, too, says Rodriguez,[7] should we act when the devil proposes certain hypothetical cases to us in order to extract a sinful consent from us, or at least to cause us to be interiorly disturbed. For example: "What would you say or what would you do if someone were to say or do such and such a thing to you?" Let us dismiss the temptation by saying: "By God's grace, I would say or do what God would want me to say or do." Thus, we shall free ourselves from imperfection and harassment.

St. Alphonsus rightly identifies this tendency and temptation to project into the future and construct scenarios that cause anxiety and preoccupation with unknowns. The fear-porn industry—news—is all too happy to fuel this anxiety to keep you coming back for more. The world, the flesh, and the devil are constantly at work to draw us out of the

---

[7] Perhaps St. Alphonsus Rodriguez (1532–1617), who was one of the first Jesuits. He was known for his obedience and discipline and suffered from scrupulosity, temptations, and attacks from the devil.

present moment, which is the only place in which we can know God's peace and presence. The devil tries to draw us into the past to be held in bondage to our shame or into the future to be fearful of possible outcomes. Thus, temptations to dwell in the past or in the future should always be resisted.

3. *In defect of body and mind.* Let us not lament if we suffer from some natural defect of body or mind—from poor memory, slowness of understanding, little ability, lameness, or general bad health. What claim have we, or what obligation is God under, to give us a more brilliant mind or a more robust body? Who is ever offered a gift and then lays down the conditions upon which he will accept it? Let us thank God for what, in His pure goodness, He has given us, and let us be content, too, with the manner in which He has given it to us. Who knows? Perhaps if God had given us greater talent, better health, a more personable appearance, we might have lost our souls! Great talent and knowledge have caused many to be puffed up with the idea of their own importance, and in their pride, they have despised others. How easily those who have these gifts fall into grave danger to their salvation! How many, on account of physical beauty or robust health, have plunged headlong into a life of debauchery! How many, on the contrary, who, by reason of poverty, infirmity, or physical deformity, have become saints and have saved their souls—who, given health, wealth, or physical attractiveness, had else lost their souls! Let us

then be content with what God has given us. *But one thing is necessary*, and it is not beauty, not health, not talent. It is the salvation of our immortal souls.

4. *In corporal infirmities.* It is especially necessary that we be resigned in corporal infirmities. We should willingly embrace them in the manner and for the length of time that God wills. We ought to make use of the ordinary remedies in time of sickness—such is God's will; but if they are not effective, let us unite ourselves to God's will, and this will be better for us than would be our restoration to health. Let us say: "Lord, I wish neither to be well nor to remain sick; I want only what Thou wilt." Certainly, it is more virtuous not to repine in times of painful illness; still and all, when our sufferings are excessive, it is not wrong to let our friends know what we are enduring and also to ask God to free us from our sufferings. Let it be understood, however, that the sufferings here referred to are actually excessive. It often happens that some, on the occasion of a slight illness or even a slight indisposition, want the whole world to stand still and sympathize with them in their illnesses. But where it is a case of real suffering, we have the example of our Lord, who, at the approach of His bitter Passion, made known His state of soul to His disciples, saying, *My soul is sorrowful even unto death* and besought His eternal Father to deliver Him from it: *Father, if it be possible, let this chalice pass from me.* But our Lord likewise taught us what we should do when we have made such a petition, when He added, *Nevertheless, not as I will, but as You will.*

How childish the pretense of those who protest that they wish for health not to escape suffering but to serve our Lord better by being able to observe their Rule, to serve the community, go to church, receive Communion, do penance, study, and work for souls in the confessional and in the pulpit.

Devout soul, tell me, why do you desire to do these things? To please God? Why, then, search any further to please God when you are sure God does not wish these prayers, Communions, penances, or studies, but He does wish that you suffer patiently this sickness He sends you? Unite, then, your sufferings to those of our Lord.

The reader might ask, "How exactly can I unite my sufferings with the suffering of Jesus?" The first step is to make an act of faith, which then turns into a prayer. An act of faith is simply a decision, based on faith, to trust God and conform your heart and mind to His will. The resulting prayer might sound something like this: "Lord, I embrace this suffering for love of You and Your holy will. Please join my suffering to Yours for the salvation of the world." To be more specific and to draw closer to the Lord, you might meditate on how your suffering, in some small way, mirrors the sufferings of Jesus.

As an example, most people who have lived long lives have been falsely accused of something at some point. If that is your suffering, meditate on the reality that Jesus, in contrast to you, deserved nothing but praise and adulation. Instead, He was falsely accused and thus endured a torture that no man could know because He was perfect love and perfect innocence.

In the moment of your suffering or your pain, you can imagine some aspect of Jesus' suffering and draw nearer to Him because your suffering has allowed you to know more about Him than if you had not suffered at all. In that moment, you can express your sorrow for His suffering and console His heart. The prayer could be something like this: "Dear Jesus, I am deeply sorry that You were falsely accused. You deserve nothing but love and adulation. I am a sinner, but I, too, have been falsely accused. In this suffering, I desire to draw near to You and to join with You in pardoning my accuser, since it is not likely that my accuser really understands what he is doing. So You said about those who crucified You! Please take my suffering and join it with Yours for the salvation of the world."

Another example comes from my life. I suffer with severe asthma—a type that results in about thirty-five hundred deaths each year. Once, when I was experiencing days of difficulty in breathing, it seemed that the Holy Spirit prompted me to unite my suffering to Jesus in a more specific way. I was drawn to consider His suffering on the Cross. Many are unaware that those who are crucified actually die of asphyxiation. Once Jesus could no longer push His body up with His feet, He could no longer inhale or exhale. In my meditation, I imagined His loss of breath and His great agony from the thousands of wounds inflicted upon Him. Then I

imagined looking into His eyes and seeing His sorrow
as He fought to raise His body up again to breathe.
This pushed against the nails in His feet and pulled
against those in His hands. The raw flesh on His back
rubbed against the Cross as He struggled to breathe.
Tears flowed from my eyes as I shared my deep sorrow
for my sin, which caused His pain and suffering. I expressed sadness that He was suffering too. I can know
only a sliver of a sliver of an iota of His suffering, but I
can know what I can know, and I can exercise my will
to turn to Him, console Him, and thank God that I
am able to know Him in this way. Thank God for the
gift of this disease that helps me to know Him in ways
that I otherwise could not.

"But," you say, "I do not want to be sick for then I am
useless, a burden to my Order, to my monastery." But
if you are united to and resigned to God's will, you will
realize that your superiors are likewise resigned to the
dispositions of divine providence and that they recognize
the fact that you are a burden not through indolence
but by the will of God. Ah, how often these desires and
these laments are born not of the love of God but of
the love of self! How many of them are so many pretexts
for fleeing the will of God! Do we want to please God?
When we find ourselves confined to our sickbed, let us
utter this one prayer: "Thy will be done." Let us repeat
this prayer time and time again, and it will please God
more than all our mortifications and devotions. There

is no better way to serve God than cheerfully to embrace His holy will.

St. John of Ávila once wrote to a sick priest: "My dear friend, do not weary yourself planning what you would do if you were well, but be content to be sick for as long as God wishes. If you are seeking to carry out God's will, what difference should it make to you whether you are sick or well?" The saint was perfectly right, for God is glorified not by our works but by our resignation to, and by our union with, His holy will. In this respect, St. Francis de Sales used to say we serve God better by our sufferings than by our actions. Many times, it will happen that proper medical attention or effective remedies will be lacking or even that the doctor will not rightly diagnose our case. In such instances, we must unite ourselves to the divine will, which thus disposes of our physical health.

The story is told of a devotee of St. Thomas of Canterbury[8] who, being sick, went to the saint's tomb to obtain a cure. He returned home cured. But then he thought to himself: "Suppose it would be better for my soul's salvation if I remained sick. What point, then, is there in being well?" In this frame of mind, he went back and asked the saint to intercede with God that He grant what would be best for his eternal salvation. His illness returned, and he was perfectly content with the

---

[8] St. Thomas of Canterbury (ca. 1118–1170), also known as Thomas à Becket, was archbishop of Canterbury and chancellor of King Henry II and was martyred in his cathedral. His shrine became a popular place of pilgrimage and miracles.

turn things had taken, being fully persuaded that God had thus disposed of him for his own good.

There is a similar account by Surio[9] to the effect that a certain blind man obtained the restoration of his sight by praying to St. Bedasto, the bishop. Thinking the matter over, he prayed again to his heavenly patron, but this time with the purpose that if the possession of his sight were not expedient for his soul, that his blindness should return. And that is exactly what happened—he was blind again. Therefore, in sickness it is better that we seek neither sickness nor health but that we abandon ourselves to the will of God so that He may dispose of us as He wishes. However, if we decide to ask for health, let us do so at least always resigned and with the proviso that our bodily health may be conducive to the health of our soul. Otherwise, our prayer will be defective and will remain unheard because our Lord does not answer prayers made without resignation to His holy will. Sickness is the acid test of spirituality because it discloses whether our virtue is real or sham.

> "Sickness is the acid test of spirituality." This is a striking statement. Why is sickness the acid test and not the depth or plentitude of voluntary penances? The reason is that we know that we can stop voluntary penances anytime we want to.

[9] Perhaps Laurentius Surius (1523–1578), who was a German Carthusian hagiographer and Church historian.

This provides a kind of psychological relief even if the penances are severe. Illness, on the other hand, like any difficult circumstance that is out of our direct control, cannot be turned off by a simple choice. Hence, to endure patiently a mild sickness is more heroic than to endure patiently a severe penance.

If the soul is not agitated, does not break out in lamentations, is not feverishly restless in seeking a cure, but instead is submissive to the doctors and to superiors, is serene and tranquil, completely resigned to God's will, it is a sign that that soul is well grounded in virtue.

What of the whiner who complains of lack of attention? That his sufferings are beyond endurance? That the doctor does not know his business? What of the fainthearted soul who laments that the hand of God is too heavy upon him? This story by St. Bonaventure in his *Life of St. Francis* is on point: On a certain occasion when the saint was suffering extraordinary physical pain, one of his religious, meaning to sympathize with him, said in his simplicity: "My Father, pray to God that He treat you a little more gently, for His hand seems heavy upon you just now." Hearing this, St. Francis strongly resented the unhappy remark of his well-meaning brother, saying: "My good brother, did I not know that what you have just said was spoken in all simplicity, without realizing the implication of your words, I should never see you again because of your rashness in passing judgment on the dispositions of divine providence." Whereupon, weak and wasted as he was by his illness, he got out of bed, knelt down, kissed the floor, and prayed thus: "Lord, I thank You for the sufferings You are sending me. Send me more, if it be Your good pleasure. My pleasure is that You afflict me and spare me not, for the fulfillment of Your holy will is the greatest consolation of my life."

Questions for Reflection

- What stood out, struck you, or moved you in this chapter?
- What in your life causes you the greatest suffering?
- Do you notice a difference between how you deal with suffering you can't control and how you deal with suffering you can control?
- Are there specific ways you can offer up your suffering and join that suffering with that of Jesus? If so, how will you do that? Be sure to write down your commitment to do this on a daily basis.

6

Spiritual Desolation

We ought to view in the light of God's holy will the loss of persons who are helpful to us in a spiritual or material way. Pious souls often fail in this respect by not being resigned to the dispositions of God's holy will. Our sanctification comes fundamentally and essentially from God, not from spiritual directors. When God sends us a spiritual director, He wishes us to use him for our spiritual profit; but if He takes him away, He wants us to remain calm and unperturbed and to increase our confidence in His goodness by saying to Him: "Lord, You have given me this help, and now You take it away. Blessed be Your holy will! I beg You, teach me what I must do to serve You."

In this manner, too, we should receive whatever other crosses God sends us. "But," you reply, "these sufferings are really punishments." The answer to that remark is: Are not the punishments God sends us in this life also graces and benefits? Our offenses against God must be atoned for somehow, either in this life or in the next. Hence, we should all make St. Augustine's prayer our own: "Lord, here cut, here burn and spare me not, but spare me in eternity!" Let us say with Job: "Let this be my comfort, that afflicting me with sorrow, He spare not." Having merited Hell for our sins, we should be consoled that God chastises us in this life and should stir ourselves to look upon such treatment as a pledge that God wishes to spare us in the next.

When God sends us punishments, let us say with the high priest Heli: *It is the Lord: let Him do what is good in His sight.* The time of spiritual desolation is also a time for being resigned.

This wisdom is worth pause and meditation: "Having merited Hell for our sins, we should be consoled that God chastises us in this life and should stir ourselves to look upon such treatment as a pledge that God wishes to spare us in the next." Our suffering, even the suffering of punishment or correction, is a revelation of God's love for us. Our suffering is God's promise. This promise and this love reveal that He desires us to be in Heaven and generously provides us with the means to get there. When we yield to and embrace these means, we yield to and embrace God. If we yield to and embrace all that God provides, we will know salvation in the next life and peace and joy in the midst of the storms of this life.

When a soul begins to cultivate the spiritual life, God usually showers His consolations upon her to wean her away from the world; but when He sees her making solid progress, He withdraws His hand to test her and to see if she will love and serve Him without the reward of sensible consolations.

Those formed in the Ignatian tradition of discernment of spirits might become confused here. The astute reader might ask, "If I am supposed to yield to suffering, and desolation is suffering, am I supposed to yield to desolation itself?" The answer is both simple and complex. No, we are not to yield to desolation but are to fight it, as indicated by St. Ignatius, by turning to God in prayer, penance, and examination. We should consider what He is doing in such circumstances. However, to add the dimension of St. Alphonsus's wisdom, we fight the desolation with a peaceful resignation to whatever the outcome of our efforts might be, as with Jesus in the Garden of Gethsemane. It is in the simultaneous movements of struggle coupled with yielding that we, like Jesus, will discover the will of God and embrace it.

The key is this: all that we do, we do with detachment from outcomes. We leave the results up to God, and we embrace whatever blessing or difficulty He decides we need. If it is a blessing of consolation or something easier, we rejoice and praise and thank Him. If it is a blessing of a difficult outcome, we rejoice and praise and thank Him.

"In this life," as St. Teresa used to say, "our lot is not to enjoy God but to do His holy will." And again, "Love of God does not consist in experiencing His tendernesses but in serving Him with resolution and humility." And in yet another place, "God's true lovers are discovered in times of aridity and temptation." Let the soul thank God when she experiences His loving-kindness, but let her not repine when she finds herself left in desolation. It is important to lay great stress on this point, because some souls, beginners in the spiritual life, finding themselves in spiritual aridity, think God has abandoned them or that the spiritual life is not for them; thus, they give up the practice of prayer and lose what they have previously gained.

Some of St. Teresa of Ávila's most stern and vehement admonitions are that we persevere in mental prayer, come what may. She knew what St. Alphonsus knew as well: that this perseverance is itself an act of love that will always receive its reward. Both Doctors warn that if we wane in the practice of prayer, we will most surely lose our footing and fall off the narrow path to Heaven.

As for aridity, we can understand it as a sense of dryness or the absence of the consoling presence of God. The key to a right perspective regarding aridity is that how we feel has nothing to do with whether God is close to or far away from us. St. John of the Cross argues that the holy soul in aridity is often closer to God than when it is in consolation. It is notable to consider that the enemy will seek to convince us, through our feelings, of the exact opposite of what is true in this case.

The time of aridity is the best time to practice resignation to God's holy will. I do not say you will feel no pain in seeing yourself deprived of the sensible presence of God; it is impossible for the soul not to feel it and lament over it, when even our Lord cried out on the Cross: *My God, my God, why have You forsaken me?*

Here again this great Doctor of souls provides a bit of relief to the reader who thinks, "How is this all possible? It's as if he is asking me to be a robot and feel nothing in all of life's trials." Nothing could be further from the truth. St. Alphonsus refers to Jesus' deep suffering on the Cross. It isn't that we don't feel these trials—we can and will always feel them. The question is: How will we respond to how we feel? Will our feelings dictate our response? Or will we exercise our will to face the difficulty with God's help, maintain our resignation to His holy will, and remain in His holy embrace?

At the time of this publication, American culture has fallen apart. It gives us advice that is exactly opposed to St. Alphonsus's. The culture tells us: If you don't like someone, replace that person. That includes yourself! If you get tired of your spouse, get a divorce. If you don't want a baby, get an abortion. If you're uncomfortable being a boy, try being a girl. If you feel it, it must be true.

But our faith calls us to love God, first by recognizing His truth with our minds and then by bringing into concert with that truth our wills and our lower nature. We embrace God out of love of Him and His truth; we order our will to that truth, and our feelings follow.

This approach will allow the wisdom of St. Alphonsus's teachings to transform us. Here we are confronted with a different vision of suffering. Will we allow our intellects to be formed by it? Will we ascent to it as truth? If we do, and we remind ourselves of it regularly, we will find that our minds begin to see and think differently. Then we must choose to respond differently. This is the ordering of our will to our intellect and to all that is true. As we do this, our emotions will typically follow, and they will eventually be formed in truth as well. As we pursue all of this out of love for God and His will, He meets us in this suffering and brings us to peace and joy, no matter the storm. He heals us through the divine surgery of suffering. He transforms us into our highest calling to love and union with Him.

In her sufferings, however, the soul should always be resigned to God's will. The saints have all experienced desolations and abandonment of soul. "How impervious to things spiritual, my heart!" cries St. Bernard. "No savor in pious reading, no pleasure in meditation or in prayer!" For the most part, it has been the common lot of the saints to encounter aridities; sensible consolations were the exceptions. Such things are rare occurrences granted to untried souls so that they may not halt on the road to sanctity; the real delights and happiness that will constitute their reward are reserved for Heaven.

This earth is a place of merit that is acquired by suffering; Heaven is a place of reward and happiness. Hence, in this life, the saints neither desired nor sought the joys of sensible fervor but, rather, the fervor of the spirit toughened in the crucible of suffering. "Oh, how much better it is," says St. John of Ávila, "to endure aridity and temptation by God's will than to be raised to the heights of contemplation without God's will!"

But you say you would gladly endure desolation if you were certain that it comes from God, but you are tortured by the anxiety that your desolation comes by your own fault and is a punishment for your tepidity. Very well, let us suppose you are right; then get rid of your tepidity and exercise more diligence in the affairs of your soul. But because you are possibly experiencing spiritual darkness, are you going to get all twisted up, give up prayer, and thus make things twice as bad as they are?

Let us assume that this aridity is a punishment for your tepidity. Was it not God who sent it? Accept your desolation as your just deserts and unite yourself to God's holy will. Did you not say that you merited Hell? And now you are complaining? Perhaps you think God should send you consolations! Away with such ideas, and be patient under

God's hand. Take up your prayers again and continue to walk in the way you have entered upon; for the future, fear lest such laments come from too little humility and too little resignation to the will of God. Therefore, be resigned and say: "Lord, I accept this punishment from Thy hands, and I accept it for as long as it pleases You; if it be Your will that I should be thus afflicted for all eternity, I am satisfied." Such a prayer, though hard to make, will be far more advantageous to you than the sweetest sensible consolations.

It is well to remember, however, that aridity is not always a chastisement; at times, it is a disposition of divine providence for our greater spiritual profit and to keep us humble. Lest St. Paul become vain on account of the spiritual gifts he had received, the Lord permitted him to be tempted to impurity: *And lest the greatness of the revelations should exalt me, there was given me a sting of my flesh, an angel of Satan to buffet me.* Prayer made amid sensible devotion is not much of an achievement: *There is a friend, a companion at the table, and he will not abide in the day of distress.* You would not consider the casual guest at your table a friend, but only him who assists you in your need without thought of benefit to himself. When God sends spiritual darkness and desolation, His true friends are known.

Palladius, the author of the *Lives of the Fathers of the Desert*, experiencing great disgust in prayer, went seeking advice from the abbot Macarius. The saintly abbot gave him this counsel: "When you are tempted in times of dryness to give up praying because you seem to be wasting your time, say: 'Since I cannot pray, I will be satisfied just to remain on watch here in my cell for the love of Jesus Christ!'" Devout soul, you do the same when you are tempted to give up prayer just because you seem to be getting nowhere. Say: "I am going to stay here just to please God."

> This is golden advice. Just remain as you are in your struggles for the sake of pleasing God. Remain with Him in your distractions. Remain with Him in your aridities. Remain with Him in your struggles, and as you do, though your feelings will not tell you the truth about what is happening, what is truly happening is that you will be transformed in and through your suffering and will acquire a deeper knowledge and love of Him.

St. Francis de Sales used to say that if we do nothing else but banish distractions and temptations in our prayers, the prayer is well made. Tauler states that persevering prayer in time of dryness will receive greater grace than prayer made amid great sensible devotion. Rodriguez cites the case of a person who persevered forty years in prayer despite aridity and experienced great spiritual strength as a result of it; on occasion, when, through aridity, he would omit meditation, he felt spiritually weak and incapable of good deeds. St. Bonaventure and

Gerson[10] both say that persons who do not experience the recollection they would like to have in their meditations often serve God better than they would do if they did have it; the reason is that lack of recollection keeps them more diligent and humble; otherwise, they would become puffed up with spiritual pride and grow tepid, vainly believing they had reached the summit of sanctity.

> What a gift those who tend to pride receive in this withholding of spiritual consolations! What a loving God, who knows we must be protected from thinking that we are the cause of our spiritual progress!

What has been said of dryness holds true of temptations also. Certainly, we should strive to avoid temptations; but if God wishes that we be tempted against faith, purity, or any other virtue, we should not give in to discouraging lamentations but should submit ourselves with resignation to God's holy will.

St. Paul asked to be freed from temptations to impurity and our Lord answered him, saying: *My grace is sufficient for thee.* So should we act when we find ourselves victims of unrelenting temptations and God seemingly

---

[10] Perhaps Jean Charlier de Gerson (1363-1429), who was a French scholar, educator, reformer, and poet, chancellor of the University of Paris, and a prominent theologian at the Council of Constance.

deaf to our prayers. Let us then say: "Lord, do with me, let happen to me, what You will; Your grace is sufficient for me. Only never let me lose this grace." Consent to temptation, not temptation of itself, can make us lose the grace of God. Temptation resisted keeps us humble, brings us greater merit, makes us have frequent recourse to God, thus preserving us from offending Him, and unites us more closely to Him in the bonds of His holy love.

Finally, we should be united to God's will in regard to the time and manner of our death. One day St. Gertrude, while climbing up a small hill, lost her footing and fell into a ravine below. After her companions had come to her assistance, they asked her if, while falling, she had any fear of dying without the sacraments. She answered:

> I earnestly hope and desire to have the benefit of the sacraments when death is at hand; still, to my way of thinking, the will of God is more important. I believe that the best disposition I could have to die a happy death would be to submit myself to whatever God would wish in my regard. For this reason, I desire whatever kind of death God will be pleased to send me.

In his *Dialogues*, St. Gregory tells of a certain priest, Santolo by name, who was captured by the Vandals and condemned to death. The barbarians told him to choose the manner of his death. He refused, saying: "I am in God's hands, and I gladly accept whatever kind of death

He wishes me to suffer at your hands; I wish no other."
This reply was so pleasing to God that He miraculously
stayed the hand of the executioner ready to behead him.
The barbarians were so impressed by the miracle that they
freed their prisoner. As regards the manner of our death,
therefore, we should esteem that the best kind of death
for us is that which God has designed for us.

When, therefore, we think of our death, let our prayer
be: "O Lord, only let me save my soul, and I leave the
manner of my death to You!" We should likewise unite
ourselves to God's will when the moment of death is near.

What else is this earth but a prison where we suffer
and where we are in constant danger of losing God?
Hence David prayed: "Bring my soul out of prison." St.
Teresa, too, feared losing God, and when she would hear
the striking of the clock, she would find consolation in
the thought that the passing of the hour was an hour
less of the danger of losing God. St. John of Ávila was
convinced that every right-minded person should desire
death on account of living in peril of losing divine grace.
What can be more pleasant or desirable than, by dying
a good death, to have the assurance of no longer being
able to lose the grace of God?

Perhaps you will answer that you have as yet done
nothing to deserve this reward. If it were God's will that
your life should end now, what would you be doing, living on here against His will? Who knows—you might fall
into sin and be lost! Even if you escaped mortal sin, you
could not live free from all sin. "Why are we so tenacious

of life," exclaims St. Bernard, "when the longer we live, the more we sin?" A single venial sin is more displeasing to God than all the good works we can perform.

> Often this lack of desire for Heaven is rooted in a failure to follow the Church's prompting to an annual reflection on death, judgment, Heaven, and Hell. How should we reflect on Heaven? For me, there is one passage in the book of Revelation that sums it all up and causes me to long for Heaven: "He will wipe every tear from their eyes. Death will be no more; mourning and crying and pain will be no more" (21:4). Even so, the escape from all that ails us is nothing to be compared with the glory of coming face-to-face with our Redeemer.

Moreover, the person who has little desire for Heaven shows he has little love for God. The true lover desires to be with his beloved. We cannot see God while we remain here on earth; hence, the saints have yearned for death so that they might go and behold their beloved Lord, face-to-face. "Oh, that I might die and behold thy beautiful face!" sighed St. Augustine. And St. Paul: *Having a desire to be dissolved and to be with Christ.* And, *When shall I come and appear before the face of God?* exclaimed the psalmist.

A hunter one day heard the voice of a man singing most sweetly in the forest. Following the sound, he came upon a leper horribly disfigured by the ravages of his disease. Addressing him, he said: "How can you sing when you are so terribly afflicted and your death is so near at hand?"

And the leper: "Friend, my poor body is a crumbling wall, and it is the only thing that separates me from my God. When it falls, I shall go forth to God. Time for me is indeed fast running out, so every day I show my happiness by lifting my voice in song."

Lastly, we should unite ourselves to the will of God as regards our degree of grace and glory. True, we should esteem the things that make for the glory of God, but we should show the greatest esteem for those that concern the will of God. We should desire to love God more than the seraphs but not to a degree higher than God has destined for us. St. John of Ávila says:

> I believe every saint has had the desire to be higher in grace than he actually was. However, despite this, their serenity of soul always remained unruffled. Their desire for a greater degree of grace sprang not from a consideration of their own good, but of God's. They were content with the degree of grace God had meted out for them, though actually God had given them less. They considered it a greater sign of true love of God to be content with what God had given them than to desire to have received more.

This means, as Rodriguez explains it, we should be diligent in striving to become perfect, so that tepidity and laziness may not serve as excuses for some to say: "God must help me; I can do only so much for myself."

Nevertheless, when we do fall into some fault, we should not lose our peace of soul and union with the will of God, which permits our fall; nor should we lose our courage. Let us rise at once from this fall, penitently humbling ourselves, and by seeking greater help from God, let us continue to march resolutely on the highway of the spiritual life.

> The enemy of our souls tempts us to sin. Then he berates us for our sin, seeking to amplify our shame. We must never fall into the trap of self-pity, anger, or any kind of self-focus when we sin. Our shame and self-focus prohibit us from turning to the One who can and will heal and restore us, and so we find no remedy for sin. When we fall, we should say, "I thank You, Lord, that I know my sin. I thank You that I know my Redeemer. Forgive me. Help me never to sin against You again. Help me to rise and focus on loving and serving You and those You have placed in my care."

Likewise, we may well desire to be among the seraphs in Heaven, not for our own glory but for God's, and to love Him more; still, we should be resigned to His will and be content with that degree of glory that, in His mercy, He intends for us. It would be a serious defect to desire the gifts of supernatural prayer—specifically, ecstasies, visions, and revelations. The masters of the spiritual life say that souls thus favored by God should ask Him to take them away so that they may love Him out of pure faith—a way of greater security. Many have come to perfection without these supernatural gifts; the only virtues worthwhile are those that draw the soul to holiness of life—namely, the virtue of uniformity with God's holy will. If God does not wish to raise us to the heights of perfection and glory, let us unite ourselves in all things to His holy will, asking Him, in His mercy, to grant us our soul's salvation. If we act in this manner, the reward that we shall receive from the hands of God, who loves, above all others, souls resigned to His holy will, will not be slight.

Questions for Reflection

- What stood out, struck you, or moved you in this chapter?
- Have you seen past troubles as afflictions or punishments that you now better understand as the benevolent providence of God? What are they? How can you avoid falling into such misunderstandings in the future?
- Have you suffered aridity in prayer? How does St. Alphonsus's wisdom help you better understand it? What can you do the next time you find yourself in aridity?
- Do you recognize God's work in providing challenges that help you avoid pride and self-sufficiency? How so?
- Do you long for Heaven? Why or why not? What needs to change for you to develop this holy yearning?
- Do you fear death? Why or why not? What is this fear rooted in?

7

Conclusion

Finally, we should consider the events that are happening to us now and that will happen to us in the future as coming from the hands of God. Everything we do should be directed to this one end: to do the will of God and to do it solely for the reason that God wills it. To walk more securely on this road, we must depend on the guidance of our superiors in external matters and on our spiritual directors in internal matters, to learn from them God's will in our regard, having great faith in the words of our Lord: *He that hears you, hears me.*

Above all, let us bend all our energies to serve God in the way He wishes. This remark is made so that we may avoid the mistake of him who wastes his time in idle daydreaming. Such a one says, "If I were to become a hermit, I would become a saint" or "If I were to enter a monastery, I would practice penance" or "If I were to go away from here, leaving friends and companions, I would devote long hours to prayer." If, if, if—all these ifs!

In the meantime, such a person goes from bad to worse. These idle fancies are often temptations of the devil because they are not in accord with God's will. Hence, we should dismiss them summarily and rouse ourselves to serve God only in the way that He has marked out for us. Doing His holy will, we shall certainly become holy in those surroundings in which He has placed us. Let us will always and ever only what God wills; for so doing, He will press us to his heart.

To this end, let us familiarize ourselves with certain texts of Sacred Scripture that invite us to unite ourselves constantly with the divine will: *Lord, what will You have me do?* Tell me, my God, what will You have me do, that I may will it also, with all my heart. *I am Yours, save me.* I am no longer my own; I am Yours, O Lord; do with me as You will. If some particularly crashing misfortune comes upon us—for example, the death of a relative, loss of goods—let us say: *Yes, Father, for so it has seemed good in Your sight.* Yes, my God and my Father, so be it, for such is Your good pleasure.

Above all, let us cherish that prayer of our Lord, which He Himself taught us: *Your will be done on earth as it is in Heaven.* Our Lord bade St. Catherine of Genoa to make a notable pause at these words whenever she said the Our Father, praying that God's holy will be fulfilled on earth with the same perfection with which the saints do it in Heaven. Let this be our practice also, and we shall certainly become saints. May the divine will be loved and praised! May the Immaculate Virgin be also praised!

Appendix A

What Next?

A significant challenge emerges when we read the writings of great saints such as Alphonsus Liguori. What is often difficult for the average reader is to understand the context and assumptions of the writer. I hope that some of the commentary has helped, but the wise reader might still ask, "What was left unsaid that is important for me to understand about the fullness of this journey to God?" This book has focused on exploring St. Alphonsus's wisdom and perspective on how God moves in and through the circumstances of life to heal us and draw us to union with Him. But now that you have finished the book, what next? What specific steps can you take in light of this new, exciting, but perhaps also overwhelming awareness of these truths of the spiritual life? How can you put this wisdom to work in your life?

Following are several recommendations for the soul who is truly motivated to put in the effort necessary to experience the profound spiritual breakthroughs and to progress more surely along the path revealed by St. Alphonsus:

1. St. Alphonsus assumes that his readers know the value of mental prayer and practice it daily. Frankly, what he proposes is exceedingly difficult, if not impossible, when we don't dedicate time to spend with Jesus in mental prayer *every single day.*

Years ago, I was inspired to help people to practice mental prayer, and I searched for but could not find a book that was simple, straightforward, and easy to implement. So I wrote the book *Into the Deep: Finding Peace through Prayer.* Pick up this book at SpiritualDirection.com, and you will discover a foundational spiritual discipline that will help you understand how to live the wisdom offered by St. Alphonsus. (Plus, the royalty funds are committed to the poor and to spiritual works of mercy, so your purchase will help others.) While you are waiting to receive your book, you can also take a free course I provide on mental prayer at ApostoliViae.org. Even if you have some experience with prayer, I strongly recommend that you take this course.

2. If you have not already done so, begin to make a daily examen, or examination of conscience, to assess your movements toward or away from God during the day with respect to the discipline of embracing His will in all things. As you answered the questions at the end of each chapter, you gained some clarity regarding how you resist

God's will and how you might better embrace it on a daily basis. Take a few of those things that you struggle with the most, and begin to practice the opposite behaviors. Consider tracking in a journal your progress and goals for growth in embracing the will of God. This will be a valuable tool to bring with you to meetings with your spiritual director, and it can assist you in preparing your plan of love (or rule of life) and in making solid confessions. We also have a free course at ApostoliViae.org on how to do this in detail.

3. Increase your participation in the sacraments of the Eucharist and Penance. Try to receive the sacrament of Penance at least once each month. Souls truly intent on traversing the narrow way should also receive the Eucharist as often as possible. Strive for more than just the Sunday obligation as your circumstances and state of life allow.

4. In addition to these spiritual disciplines, the daily practice of discernment of spirits is extremely powerful in helping you to identify when desolation tries to draw you out of a state of gratitude and the embrace of God's will. See my book *Spiritual Warfare and the Discernment of Spirits* at SpiritualDirection.com and the free course at ApostoliViae.org.

5. Learn and follow the Paradigm of Ascent as outlined below, and take the free course on this topic on ApostoliViae.org.

The Paradigm of Ascent as a Pathway Forward

St. Alphonsus never intended *Uniformity with God's Will* to be read by those who could not understand it because they were not yet practicing foundational spiritual disciplines. Yes, his work is meant for all to understand, but it cannot be understood fully by those who simply read the book as an intellectual exercise rather than using it as a guide for the journey that he assumes the reader is already on!

To help you better understand the dynamics of that journey, I provide below a brief summary of what I call the Paradigm of Ascent™.[11] This framework represents the foundational practices of every saint of the past and of every holy person alive today. These are practices that St. Alphonsus assumed were in place in the life of every reader who attempted to understand and follow his wisdom regarding the embrace of God's holy will. The truths revealed in the paradigm are foundational in that if they are not all present in some substantive way in your life, a deeper understanding of the interior life will remain beyond your grasp. This is a bad thing only if you fail to take the next steps to remedy whatever deficiency you uncover.

The first foundational truth is that you must have an authentic *yes* in your heart to God to begin your journey to union with Him. It is not enough merely to know

---

[11] Note that this trademark is to ensure its proper use. It is a very simple but powerful model that can easily be trivialized by those who use it without sufficient formation behind each of its components.

about God or even to practice your Faith: you must know God intimately. This is the path of the mystics, but it is also the path every soul can know and must embrace to get to Heaven. This path is unfamiliar to many Catholics because most Catholics do not hear a pronounced or emphatic call to the constant conversion we all need. But Jesus frequently offered this call to conversion and even warnings about Hell to His closest followers. Though you have been baptized and confirmed, you still must constantly recognize your need for God and for the conversion of life that draws you ever closer to Him.

The second foundational element is the most important support for the *yes* of the heart, and it consists of the sacraments of the Eucharist and regular Confession. It is a mortal sin to miss Mass on Sunday, but beyond the threat of Hell, if you fail to fulfill your Sunday obligation, you deny yourself the Eucharist—the most powerful sustenance of your faith. Rather, you should participate in the Holy Sacrifice of the Mass as frequently as possible. The sacrament of Penance is also necessary to support your *yes*. All too often, Catholics underestimate the power of this sacrament. You might think of it merely as a remedy for sin, which it is, but it is also a great grace to strengthen you against falling into sin again. Put another way, the sacrament of Penance both provides forgiveness of sins and strengthens you in your efforts to fight sin. It is also the most significant weapon against Satan in spiritual warfare in the Church's arsenal. Regardless, if you are not reconciled to God and not living in a state of grace, you are cut off from the life of grace and will not be able to discern properly the difference between the inspirations and influence of God and the temptations and false lies of the devil. If you are not in a state of grace, you have fundamentally said *no* to God and His plan for your life and *yes* to the devil.

Because of the rampant poor catechesis of our time, I must be absolutely clear on this point. Living in a state of grace means that you are living without unconfessed mortal sins and you are following the teachings of the Church in every aspect of your life. Both the *Roman Catechism* and the modern *Catechism of the Catholic Church* are very clear on these matters and should be studied by every serious Catholic. The diagram below reveals the beginning elements of your foundation in the paradigm to ascend to greater holiness and the relationship of those elements with one another.

As I have emphasized in this book, the third foundational element to authentic discipleship is daily prayer. The most powerful daily prayers are mental prayer and the Rosary. Sts. Teresa of Ávila and Alphonsus Liguori, both Doctors of the Church, consider daily mental prayer to be necessary for salvation because of the impact on the soul of those who daily draw near to their Savior in dedicated intimacy. As mentioned previously, sound and very practical understanding of the practice of daily mental prayer can be found in my book *Into the Deep: Finding Peace through Prayer*. The Rosary, as revealed by our Blessed Mother, is necessary for both your salvation and that of the world. Together, these two daily prayers provide protection as a kind of shield and nurture your *yes*, which allows you to move forward in faith.[12] With these daily practices in place, our diagram now looks like this and begs for a final aspect necessary for balance.

The fourth foundational element to your discernment is *ascesis*. This ancient Greek word simply means "exercise." In our usage, that exercise is to exert conscious daily and deliberate effort away from sin and selfishness and toward self-giving to God and your neighbor. It is

---

[12] Whether you have yet to take up the practice of the Rosary or are a long-time practitioner and need to go deeper or break the pattern of rote familiarity, you will find helpful *The Contemplative Rosary*, which I co-authored with Connie Rossini.

the practical result of what Jesus meant when He said, "If any man would come after me, let him deny himself and take up his cross and follow me" (Matt. 16:24).

Ascesis is self-giving and self-denial—saying no to the draws of your lower nature in order to say yes to giving yourself completely to God, to His will, and to those whom He has placed in your care or in your circle of influence. Practicing ascesis daily is simply what it means to truly follow Jesus and what He meant when He said, "If you want to be my disciple, take up your cross and follow me." On an encouraging note, if you pursue the sacraments and prayer the way the saints did, your practice of ascesis is already well under way!

This final element completes what I like to call a "saint-making machine." These basic elements are in place in the life of every saint and everyone who makes progress in the spiritual life toward God and peace and away from sin and the sorrows of sin. This Paradigm of Ascent™ is also the necessary basis for beginning to distinguish between the voice and influence of God and the voice and influence of the enemy of your soul.

As you begin to implement or deepen these disciplines, you will, by God's grace and provision, lay a foundation that is, in and of itself, the most powerful healing and liberating force you can know. You will begin living by what is known in Catholic Tradition as a rule of life, or what we call in our community of Apostoli Viae, a "plan of love." A plan of love is simply a purposeful way to live and love God and those He has placed in our care. A good plan always has concrete commitments that you make to God and your loved ones on a daily, weekly, or monthly basis. A simple plan of love might look something like this:

- Daily mental prayer: wake up at 6:00 a.m. and pray for ten minutes, focusing on that day's Gospel reading for Mass.
- Daily Rosary: pray one decade on the way to work.
- Attend Mass every Sunday without fail.
- Go to Confession every other week.

The final step in your foundation is what is known as the examen, or examination of conscience. You might have heard the phrase in business "What gets measured gets done." The same principle applies in the life of the soul who truly desires to give itself to God and to know the peace and joy He has for it. It is common to hear folks shy away from the examen because they have been taught a predominantly negative approach that is solely focused on where they have failed or what they have done wrong. This is not the approach that I recommend.

Instead, I encourage practicing the examen in a way that is focused on God's redemptive power and mercy, not on your weaknesses and failures. As St. Paul recalled, "He said to me, 'My grace is sufficient for you, for my power is made perfect in weakness.' ... For when I am weak, then I am strong" (2 Cor. 12:9–10).

The approach is simple. Every night before going to bed, take five minutes to review your day. Ask the Lord and the Blessed Mother to reveal what you need to know. Then step into your "mental helicopter," fly up about twenty feet, and then fly back to when you got out of bed in the morning. Then slowly fly over your day from morning to evening, asking two simple questions:

What have I been able to do, by the grace of God, that honors Him and others? When you discover these things, express praise and thanksgiving to God. This can be as simple as "Thank You, Lord, for the ability to pray according to my plan of love when I didn't feel like doing so."

How have I failed to honor God and others? When you discover these things, continue to pray in thanksgiving, something like this: "Thank You, Lord, for revealing my sin to me so that I can be forgiven and strengthened to overcome this sin in the future. Thank You for Your promise and provision of forgiveness and strength against sin and temptation."

Now, this may seem very simple—and it is! However, don't be fooled. This powerful practice is no less important to the Christian than a compass is to the man seeking a way out of the wilderness. It keeps you awake to your progress on the narrow way to Heaven, and it helps ensure that you stay on the path. It also perfects your trust in God and deepens your understanding of yourself as a beloved child, wholly dependent on His help and mercy for every good in your life.

Appendix B

Resources for Continued Spiritual Growth

If you are ready to engage more deeply in the battle for peace and strength in the storm and to deepen your relationship with the God who longs for you, go to ApostoliViae.org and create a free profile. Once you complete that process, go to the Courses page to find a series of free mini courses on overcoming habitual sin, discernment of spirits, mental prayer, the examen, and much more.

You will also gain access to a printable summary guide for both the examen and the rules of discernment that will reinforce what you have read in this book and help you to learn and apply the powerful life-changing wisdom of St. Alphonsus Liguori.

Here are additional recommended resources to help you on your journey.

Spiritual Warfare and the Discernment of Spirits by Dan Burke provides a foundational understanding of the battleground of the mind, how the enemy works in this area to keep us in desolation and lead us to sin and the rejection of God's will, and how Scripture and the wisdom of St. Ignatius of Loyola can help you fight back against the world, the flesh, and the devil and win. (SpiritualDirection.com)

The Devil in the Castle: St. Teresa of Avila, Spiritual Warfare, and the Progress of the Soul by Dan Burke provides a deep reflection on the wisdom of St. Teresa of Ávila in her seminal work *The Interior Castle*, which reveals battles of each stage of the spiritual life and how to overcome them and come to union with God. (SpiritualDirection.com)

Daily Spiritual Sustenance: SpiritualDirection.com is meant to help you to grow spiritually by providing thousands of articles, videos, and other powerful materials rooted in the Magisterium and the faithful mystical tradition of the Church. Be sure to sign up for the e-mail digest, which will provide you with new insights on the journey every week.

Deep Formation in the Spiritual Life and Spiritual Theology (Avila-Institute.org): The Avila Institute for Spiritual Formation provides spiritual formation to laity, priests, and religious worldwide through live online classes. There are courses at a level for busy people as well as graduate studies for those who have the time and inclination.

Appendix C

Original Preface by Bishop Thomas W. Tobin

In volume 1, *Opere Ascetiche di S. Alfonso M. de Liguori*, Roma, 1933, *Uniformity with God's Will* is included as one of three works under the heading "Lesser Works on Divine Love." There is no preface in the Italian original. However, it has been thought well to provide one here.

Prof. Candido M. Romano says this brochure was written probably in 1755, as appears from a letter by the saint, under date of November 2, 1755, to Sr. Giannastasio at Cava. Romano goes on to say:

> This (i.e., God's will) was for Alphonsus a theme of predilection, a theme dearest to his heart. Just as St. Ignatius stressed "the greater glory of God," St. Alphonsus in all his works, gave prominence to "the greater good pleasure of God." Most likely the occasion that brought forth this treatise was the death, in 1753, of Father Paul Cafaro, C.Ss.R., St. Alphonsus's confessor and director. The death of this worthy priest deeply affected the saint, and

he expressed his sentiments in a poem on God's will. The wide acclaim it received may have suggested to him the thought that a tract on the same subject would be helpful to the souls of others. If this be true, his surmise proved correct, for the appearance of his subsequent pamphlet was greeted with instant favor.

Cardinal Villecourt, in his *Life of St. Alphonsus*, quotes long passages from this pamphlet and ends by saying: "Our Saint frequently read it himself and when his sight had failed, he arranged to have it read to him by others."

This brochure bears the stamp of Alphonsian simplicity of style and solidity of doctrine. Moreover, the instances he cites from the lives of the saints have a gentle graciousness and contain a fragrance that is redolent of the *Fioretti of St. Francis of Assisi*.

Through God's grace and our Lady's prayers, may a diligent reading of the book bring us far along the way of perfection by the cultivation of uniformity with God's holy will!

—Thomas W. Tobin, C.Ss.R.
October 16, 1952
Feast of St. Gerard Majella, C.Ss.R.

About the Authors

St. Alphonsus Liguori

St. Alphonsus was born into the noble house of Liguori in 1696. Well educated and talented from an early age, he studied law at the University of Naples and received his doctorate when he was only sixteen. He earned success as a lawyer, eventually becoming one of the leaders of the Neapolitan Bar. A turning point came in Alphonsus's life, however, when he overlooked a point in a case that rendered his entire argument unsound. Crushed and humiliated by this mistake, he abandoned the practice of law, never to return. This incident showed the young lawyer the vanity and folly of worldly affairs, and he resolved to dedicate his life entirely to God.

Despite his father's bitter opposition, Alphonsus entered the priesthood and was ordained in 1726. In 1732, he founded the Congregation of the Most Holy Redeemer, also known as the Redemptorists. He was made a bishop in 1762.

Alphonsus vowed never to waste a moment of his time, and he fulfilled this promise to a heroic degree. "I never remember," said one of his companions, "to have seen Alphonsus waste a moment when he lived with us. He was always preaching, or hearing confessions, or at prayer or study." Alphonsus wrote more than a hundred books. He died in 1787 and was declared a Doctor of the Church by Pope Pius IX in 1871.

Alphonsus was filled with a great zeal for souls. His eloquent sermons, wise teachings, and kindness as a confessor won many souls for Christ. "In God you possess the most exalted and supreme Lord," he wrote in his book *How to Pray at All Times* (1753), "but also a Friend who loves you with the greatest possible love. He is not offended — on the contrary He is pleased — when you treat Him with that confidence, freedom, and tenderness with which a child treats its mother." Through his inspiring words and instructive teaching, St. Alphonsus's enduring works continue to show souls how to develop such friendship with God.

Dan Burke

Dan Burke is the founder and president of the Avila Institute for Spiritual Formation, which offers graduate and personal enrichment studies in spiritual theology to priests, deacons, religious, and laity in more than ninety countries and prepares men for seminary in more than forty dioceses.

Dan is the author or editor of more than fifteen books on authentic Catholic spirituality and with his wife, Stephanie, hosts the *Divine Intimacy Radio* show, which is broadcast weekly on EWTN Radio. Past episodes, along with thousands of articles on the interior life, can be found at SpiritualDirection.com.

In his deep commitment to the advancement of faithful Catholic spirituality, he is also the founder of Apostoli Viae, a worldwide, private association of the faithful dedicated to living and advancing the contemplative life.

Most importantly, Dan is a blessed husband, father of four, and grandfather of one—and is grateful to be Catholic.

SPIRITUAL DIRECTION
ᔒ SERIES ᔕ

SOPHIA INSTITUTE PRESS

If this book has caused a stir in your heart to continue to pursue your relationship with God, we invite you to explore two extraordinary resources, SpiritualDirection.com and the Avila Institute for Spiritual Formation.

The readers of SpiritualDirection.com reside in almost every country of the world where hearts yearn for God. It is the world's most popular English site dedicated to authentic Catholic spirituality.

The students of the Avila Institute for Spiritual Formation sit at the foot of the rich and deep well of the wisdom of the saints.

You can find more about the Avila Institute at
www.Avila-Institute.com.

Sophia Institute

Sophia Institute is a nonprofit institution that seeks to nurture the spiritual, moral, and cultural life of souls and to spread the gospel of Christ in conformity with the authentic teachings of the Roman Catholic Church.

Sophia Institute Press fulfills this mission by offering translations, reprints, and new publications that afford readers a rich source of the enduring wisdom of mankind.

Sophia Institute also operates the popular online resource CatholicExchange.com. *Catholic Exchange* provides world news from a Catholic perspective as well as daily devotionals and articles that will help readers to grow in holiness and live a life consistent with the teachings of the Church.

In 2013, Sophia Institute launched Sophia Institute for Teachers to renew and rebuild Catholic culture through service to Catholic education. With the goal of nurturing the spiritual, moral, and cultural life of souls, and an abiding respect for the role and work of teachers, we strive to provide materials and programs that are at once enlightening to the mind and ennobling to the heart; faithful and complete, as well as useful and practical.

Sophia Institute gratefully recognizes the Solidarity Association for preserving and encouraging the growth of our apostolate over the course of many years. Without their generous and timely support, this book would not be in your hands.

www.SophiaInstitute.com
www.CatholicExchange.com
www.SophiaInstituteforTeachers.org

Sophia Institute Press is a registered trademark of Sophia Institute.
Sophia Institute is a tax-exempt institution as defined by the
Internal Revenue Code, Section 501(c)(3). Tax ID 22-2548708.

A Special Thanks to the
Finding Peace in the Storm
Launch Team

Ally Brown; Natalie Hnatiw; Margaret Maggio; Margaret Cruz; Cheryl Muma; Fr. Matthew MacDonald; JoAnn Garza; Kevin P. Sinnott; Laura Daniel; Robyn Bachmann; Mary Kelly; Brenda Ripslinger; Lynette Wijnveldt; Jennifer Posey; Marianne Joines; James C Fields Jr.; Carla Hamarsnes; Wilma Drummer; April and John Mascola; Jeremy and Michele Di Piazza; Laura Baylis; Juan Tejero; Amy Nocera; Heidi Kirkpatrick Hedrick; Michael LaFramboise; Leena Joseph; Dawn Powell; Catherine Collins; Karen Davidian; Tammie Young; Deacon Rod & Cindy Reyna; Diane McCall; Cindy Loescher; Anne Louise DePalo; Lauren Whittaker; Grace Ruelle; Rose Cowell; Margaret Seguin; Anthony Kropinak.; Amy and Danny Ryan; Elisabet Aiezza; Allison Wyers; Elizabeth Plemel-Scott; Jose Grajeda; Joe Leal; Michele Kendrioski; Joe Papranec; Jesse Hinde; Selina Stabler; Peter Savino; Mitzi Phalen; Joanne Haddad; Dr. Holly Smith; Scott Surette; Mary Angela Multhauf; Andrew James Sammut; Marianne Lan; Rosemary Wilkins; Debra Brunsberg; Stefan Ulrich; Dawn Lyn Wilson; David Pryse; Melanie Burosh; Joyce Forchuk; Shawn Spinneweber; Jean Jones; Alex King; Living at facility not able to contribute LaCroix; Melissa bustillos; Jeanette Plowman; Fred Ebong; Chris Pampo; Christopher Jimenez; Joyce Iroka; Margaret Zylla; Laura Bueno; Angela Mose; Peggy Hool; Marjorie Morris; Rosemary Nabogis; Sara Magnus; Cecilia Torres; Denise Homsher; Jonathan Kelly; Sandra Kucharski; Sandra Kucharski; Sandra Kucharski; Sandra A. Kucharski; Candace MacMillan; Gilberto Loaeza; Marie Hall; Anita Sendze; Hunter Allen; Elizabeth Manning; Nicole Webb; Ann Marie Canelas; Sandra Sebastian; Bernie Bys; Razel Pasco; Gabriela Chavez; Sylvia Triche; Dr. Gerry Sotomayor; Deborah Bartlett-Karbowiak; Heidi Schneider; Sylvia Jimenez; John Sharry; Wade Ballou; Corina Scott; Richard Bourque; Theresa Cusumano; Carollyn Eagle; Lynne Amerson; Zoe Miniti; TARA STOKES; Evelyn Mogere; David Boze; Joelle Cody; Jerry Masty; Sr mercy Boateng; Chris Da Silva; John Newsham; Colleen Remein; Marianne DiBugno; Ramon III Guison; Jacob Leal; MaryAnne Moran; Peyton Phillips; Jennifer Bolster; David Lim; Cecilia Morais; Julie Moore; Mary Evans; Aisling Smith; Sofia Fountain; David Holzmer; Christy Kantack; Carolyn Schultz; Paul Jackson; Jairo Morfin; Deirdre Walsh; Rose Masone; Michele Wills; Christino Chiveza; Suzanne Sims; Priester Eustaquio; Donna Jean Marram; Meynardo (Peddy) Ascio; Donna Jean Marram; Fr. Joseph Sibilano; Pier-Olivier Arsenault; Don Miller; Nomawonga Gloria Xangathi; Tricia Zaremba; LeeAnn Gervais; David Craparotta; Vivian Anthony;

Mario Albrizio; Barbara Parrish; Emiliana Tuhoye; Kelly Pontiere; Gene
Kelly; Mary Gross; Patricia Connolly; Deborah Crosby; Jeffrey Crane;
Gloria Bautista; Michael DeWitt; Susan Busch; Diane Corlett; Bruce
Huthmacher; Bill Poska; Charles Trujillo; Linda Smallwood; Judith
Guidry; Eugene Beckman; Veronica Mora; Ed Taekema; Susanne
Moskalski; Julie Walters; Dolores Nevares; Matthew Clark; Elizabeth
Caliwara; Jean Fielding; Jennifer Brannon; Connor Searle; Theresa
Schortgen; Anthony Acosta; Raul Lanting; Norma McGuire; Joan
Bohata; Joan Callaghan; Elizabeth MacAdams; Denyse Shannon; Arlene
Williams; Jennifer Morrill-Fabrizi; Suzanne Beadles; Shirley Bachmeier;
Ivette Figueroa; Gerry Jacob; Nancy Cross; Tonya Salas; Margaret Olabisi
Mekwuye; Shirley Bachmeier; Shirley Ehlers; Teresa McReynolds;
Wendee Siebert; Annie Woodman; Susan Barclay; Mary Anne Condit;
Helen Westover; Donna Slusz; Diana O'Brien; Susan Needham;
Montana O'Reilly; Dominic and Margaret Cingoranelli; Rich Vosler;
Eileen McCoy; Edward Kentgen; Donielle Wilde; Lucia Koo; Lisa Durst;
Jessica Falke; Donielle Wilde; Nellie E Gentry; Efflyn Tandanu; John
Bowen; Cynthia Newcombe; Jerilynn Prokop; Carl Sommer; Jane
Wangari; Deacon Joseph Boyle; Donna Wittmeyer; Kevin Rilott; Rosann
Exline; Andrea Ngui; John Pendergast; Jim Nyhan; Paul Nnanwobu;
James Nguyen; Chet Stagnaro; Ryan Seeley; Alan Horlbogen; Gloria
Domenech; Katie Utter; Angela Longoria; Marie Czelusniak; Tim
Wagner; Constance Beck; Mona Patrock; Jana Ferner; Ben Floyd; Ruth
Dade; Jo Jackson; Richard Junod; Nancy Sullivan; Michael Alonzi;
Christine Rich; George Williams; Michael Pennell; Dolores Fleming; Kat
Barr; Alice Bernard; Elisa Lopez; Janet Mancusi; Anne Toffey; Crystal
Gordon; Marie Claire Bilyk; Michael Mulski; Florence Suimin;
Imaculata Marriott; Vanessa Roubideaux; Dolores Delaney; Michael
Bonin; Carolyn Brown; Alicia Formato; Thomas Rastelli; Luis Cruz;
Nera Francis; Madelyn Myers; Robert Rivell; Liz Cho Hardy; Kathy
Adams ofs; Laura Baylis; D' Jacques; Donna Cobb; Michie Leblanc;
Danilo Giribaldi; Susan De Longis; Cathie Farr; Beatriz Concepcion;
Mary Ruth Hackett; Christa Oancia; Katherine Brenner; Vanessa Edwards;
Laverne Cornett; Scott Baier; Maryann Pereira; Al and Pat Elsenpeter;
Berkeley Monroe; Carolina Martinez; Norman McFall; Kristin Priola;
Noemi Moore; Bettye Williams; Albert Lewis; David and Jennifer
Smarsh; Colleen Walker; Claudia Russell; Casimira Rodriguez; Kimberly
McCoy; Debra Wobschall; William Frederick; Tom Robertson; Dean
Rowinski; Kevin Coy; Cynthia Menne; Leasa Yoshida; Mike Fontecchio;
Yvonne Dadaya; Teresa Turner; Deb Britain; Geoff Poulter; Mary Eileen
Warfield; Mary Eileen Warfield; Pat Hanley; Mary Lawrence; Patricia
Straus; Cynthia Snider; Patrick Shannon; Mike Hansberry; Janice Hughes;
Vicki Hatfield; Suzanne Macias; AVIS Gomez; Annette Hutchison;

Angela Modarelli; Lori Sautter; Larry Garces; Vandana Maria Paul; Robert James; Keith Kelly; Ariane Chui; Monique Thérèse Willemsocds; Adriana Olmedo; Paul Dillinger; Taylor Smith; John Burke; Rosa Seib; Arliene Christison; Anita Kopriva; Arline Saiki; Tanya D'Souza; Patsy Schlaegel; Janice Hughes; Sean Warfield; Mary Stefanov; Anna Nguyen; Marie-claire Sawmy; Diane Buckley; Grace Small; Annette Wasinger; Jane Woodring; Eva Johnston; Martha Mcindoe; Beverly Nichols; Patti Forman; Jessica Pennebaker; Neville Arul Sinnappah; Michael Vogel; Brenda Bowers; Cheryl La Follette; MaryKatherine Bushey; Mary Anderson; Tom Guidry; Edgard Riba; Angela Oprendek; Jose Hernandes; Eileen Kelleher; Steven Buck; Barry Johnson; Carol Younger; Andrea Bargender; Deborah Connell; Michael Maker; Karen Bianco; Danielle Abbott; Gail Ezell; Beth Crawford; Randolph Ramos; Juan Marin; Robert Riordan; Geoff Walter; Peggy Maggio; Debra Scott; Brenda Bonvillain; Janice Triner; Damian Borda; Kathryn Frits; Denise Andrin; Evan Collins; Remi Wauthy; Sarah Holderness; Amy Shaffer; Marge Morone; Jeannie Pfeifer; Deanna Williston OFS; Evelyn Price; Janice Toledo; Anderson Lopez; Teri Hammons; James Wilson; Bernadette Lekena; Margaret Jourden; Kathy Rossi; Jose San Juan; Colleen Cronin; Jillian Wernke; Marita Bolling; Eileen Swan; Robin Sellers; Eric Duffert; Tim Burley; Joe Canzoneri; Donna Damico; Dotti Easter; Mike and Michele Mason; Lorraine Wilson; Tammie Goldschmidt; Bernadette Frederick; Roseann Gaul; Julie Scegura; Patricia Cooper; Denise Skrocki; Tracye Record; Mary Ptak; Sabestine Emepuru; Dr Joan DiGregorio; Tom Robertson; Tom Robertson; Theresa Viswanathan; John Galdes; Morgan Arcuri; Jim Miller; Juanita Morales; Paul Leader; Noreen D'Souza; Kate Raeder; Susan Mulski; Andrea Barrett; Stephen Burke; Cleo Hanna; Patricia Guerrero; Frederick Mena-Gutierrez; John Janney; Agnes nick; Penny Thibodeaux; Donnie Kron; Rita Levine; David Drake; Lynne Fischer; Mary Becker; Brian Zogg; Mary Mesquita; Lino Viola; Lisa Jones; Jackie Ranger; Meg Kinney; Maureen Adolf; Mary Hall; Lou Vallarta; Tonya Herron; Carol Ann Sahady; Charlene Szczecinski; Helen Smith; Jennifer Hermann; Shelley Thomas; Michael Wick; Marie Tomlin; John Tancik; Debbie Andruk; Lorraine Smidt; Daniel Winegarden; Lorena Wallace; Karen Burden; Ana Pesic; Esteban Negrete; Mary Zayachek; Jennifer Langer; Mary Look; Patricia Martin; Karen Bonvecchio; Lynette Wijnveldt; Laura Hoffmann; Julia Bojarski; Todd Macke; Rupa Vinod; Ana María Perdigones Tornero; Lynette Taylor; Jan Trigleth; Peter Scarpelli; Sylvia Zapien; Bernard Kurera; Diane Nicholson; Timoteo Saldaña Honesto; John Egerer; Harold Greblo; Dcn. Tierney; Arthur Manigault; Dan Goddu; Thomas Heard; Gina Nakagawa; Olguita Santiago; Jeffrey Lippert; Marie Kudela; Josephine Maseko; Jeffrey Mcgovern; Linda Delia;

Notes

Joanna Vassallo; David Alston; Bindu Anthony; Henrietta Netta; Shalee Morris; Markiemarie Works; Luis Medina; Marissa Mendoza; Michelle McLaughlin; Sharon Dragan; Mayur Fernandes; Stephanie Simmons; Laura Rogge; Joe Myers; R M Tennyson; Michael Verceles; Anita Horinek; Dave Chwalik; Pattie Stark; Karen Lewter; Ken Champagne; Leticia Mendoza; Matthew Cobb; Robert Lord; Jorge Medina; Carmella Thompson; Tiffany Good; Maria Romero; Chris Anderson; Pauline Teahan; Kevin Jordan; Diane Schwind; Christopher Stephens; Karen Turner; Cindi Cass; Mary Cauley; Lori Myers; Diep Ngo Ward; Christine Martinez; Leticia Sparkes; Daniel Grabo Sr; Margaret Brownhill; Rachel Fuhry; Lisa Campbell; Charlene Stier; Sharon Otto; Lori Guidry; Javier Rocha; Saji Sebastian; Monica Bergeron; Catherine Ranum; Christopher Baker; Raina Marciano; Patricia Tvedt; Juan Carlos Ramirez; John Brozovich; Ana Johnson; Suzi Dutro; May Respicio; Joseph and Mary Humphrey; Diann Mohammed; Brenda Conyers; Shirl Lee Hemingway; Aleksandra Blaszczyk; Patti Smith; Criselda Freasier; Genaro Garza III; Michael Maturen; John Caso; Ryan DeHaan; Marivic Torres; MaryLou Schwaner; Sarah Damm; Randy Carson; Valerie D'silva; Deborah Schopperth; Guadalupe Ramirez; Christine Ferraro; Lisa Balogh; Michele Vecchia; Diane Hoyum; Keith Rickert; Susan Moreland; Barbara Bertsch; Steve Hyatt; Katherine Gugliuzza; John Kubasak; Danny Ryan; Emma Woelfel; Sharon Vanderzyl; Robert & Melinda Sass; Bernardo D'Carmine; Ileene Lanier; Anne Keller; Kathleen Glavich, SND; Br Jerome Mary Vostan; Lamont Applegate; Joeline Chipps; Bernadette Capuyan; Samuel Benjamin Asantey; Susana Ayers; Anthony Bollino; Louis Elosta; Jillian Buhl; Tere Adams; Amanda Golec; Margaret Kepple; Barbara Lake; Gregory Ringel; Crystelle Najm; Ken Johnston; Tony Maceo; Megan Mottet; Paul Hammond; Daniel Golec; John Porea; Ken Johnston; Emilie Kua; Patricia Baynes; Rick Fortune; Reyna Sonju; Michelle Meza; Laura Archbold; Holly Parsons; Janina Duer; Judi Wicks; Susanne Houston; Dcn Francis Potts; David Albers; Sharon Patrick; David W. Warner; Dale Johnson; LeRoy M Buchholdt; Marc French; Vishal Nehra; Cheramie Dankesreiter; John Ashmore; Patricia Budd; Allen Cuzelis; Abas James ODIDI; Laura Stanosheck; Brock Cordeiro; Mark Danaho; Lynda Roucloux Kirtland; Brian Lawless; Michelle Williamson; Robert Zaar; Alexandra Kubebatu; Kate Eschbach; Laura Paradis; Jim Ryan; Anita Crosby; Oscar Diaz; Brittany Thomas; Brittany Thomas; Yanni Saratsis